Early Testimonials for Change for Good: The Transformative Power of Giving as the Ultimate Cure

"Heidi's dedication to amplifying the voices of the everyday heroes is beautiful. Celebrating the work of these beautiful humans, she inspires us all to be more compassionate, engaged, and committed to creating a more just and equitable world. I highly recommend this book to anyone seeking to be inspired, motivated, and connected to the incredible work being done in the communities we live in."
—**Maggie Kane**, Founder of A Place at the Table

I0559309

"Heidi is so much more than just an incredible woman—she's a phenomenal podcaster, a gifted writer, and a true creator of good in this world. What stands out most to me is her genuine commitment to making the world a better place. I'm beyond grateful that our paths crossed, and it's an honor to work together in our shared mission to create a positive impact."
—**Cindy Witteman**, Founder of Driving Single Parents and Host of The Little Give Show

"In 2014, I was honored to be interviewed by Heidi Johnson for Charity Matters. I fell in love with her mission and her spirit. Heidi seeks to tell the story of everyday nonprofit heroes. She is certainly one of my heroes. Few understand as Heidi does the challenges small nonprofit organizations go through to carry out their mission. I am grateful to Heidi and Charity Matters for not only highlighting UpRising Yoga's work, but for also uplifting many other heartwarming stories across our communities."
—**Jill Ippolito**, Founder of Uprising Yoga

"It is rare to find a person who is genuinely and whole-heartedly a force for good. Heidi Johnson is one such person. When faced with a tragic experience in her own life, she turned her grief into positive action, launching a nonprofit that helps countless people navigate through unimaginable loss and hardship. Becoming a nonprofit founder sparked Heidi's passion for philanthropy and storytelling. Through her platform and podcast, Charity Matters, she generously and compellingly amplifies the stories of other nonprofit founders, connecting people and causes. Charity Matters is a beacon of hope and inspiration in a sometimes dark and broken world. Her perspective and voice are clear and unimpeachable. Heidi's book Change for Good is the call to action we need in this moment - the reminder that we all have the power to transform our own lives and our collective future through the power of giving."
—**Natalie Silverstein MPH**, Nonprofit founder,
Podcast Host and philanthropist

"Heidi's writing is a powerful testament to the transformative impact of passion and purpose in the nonprofit sector. Through compelling stories and insightful reflections, she inspires and empowers readers to make a meaningful difference in the world."
—**Paige Chenault Lohoefer**, Founder of the Birthday Party Project

CHANGE
— *for* —
GOOD

THE TRANSFORMATIVE POWER OF GIVING AS THE ULTIMATE CURE

HEIDI JOHNSON

© 2024 ALL RIGHTS RESERVED.

Published by She Rises Studios Publishing **www.SheRisesStudios.com**

No part of this book may be reproduced or transmitted in any form whatsoever, electronic, or mechanical, including photocopying, recording, or by any informational storage or retrieval system without the expressed written, dated and signed permission from the publisher and author.

LIMITS OF LIABILITY/DISCLAIMER OF WARRANTY:

The author and publisher of this book have used their best efforts in preparing this material. While every attempt has been made to verify the information provided in this book, neither the author nor the publisher assumes any responsibility for any errors, omissions, or inaccuracies.

The author and publisher make no representation or warranties with respect to the accuracy, applicability, or completeness of the contents of this book. They disclaim any warranties (expressed or implied), merchantability, or for any purpose. The author and publisher shall in no event be held liable for any loss or other damages, including but not limited to special, incidental, consequential, or other damages.

ISBN: 978-1-964619-45-3

Dedication

This book is dedicated to all of the helpers who change the world for good every day and to my husband, Ron, who changes mine.

Table of Contents

Forward

It has always been my dream to write as a lifelong storyteller, connector, communicator, and believer in good. I am also a helper. I love to help. I believe if you're reading this, you are one too. How can we, as helpers make a difference? How can one person make the world better? It is a daunting and overwhelming task. Not an impossible one, of that I am sure. Like all great challenges, it starts with one tiny idea. A marathon begins with one small step, and this book begins with the first word. Your journey towards making your life better and our world better just began.

My hope for you is that after taking this first step and coming on this journey, you will see aspects of your own story in the many stories shared here. As a result, you will find ways to use the challenges you have been handed to discover your gifts, your power, and how to use them to make the world better, one tiny step at a time, in your journey to Change for Good.

As Glenda the Good Witch told Dorothy in *The Wizard of Oz* after her journey, "*You always had the power, my dear, you just had to learn it for yourself.*"

So let the journey begin...

Book Summary

If given the chance, many of us would undoubtedly change the world for the better. We would choose to eradicate war, hunger, illness, and suffering. However, the enormity of such a task can feel overwhelming, leaving us uncertain of where to begin as individuals. Yet, the truth is that each of us possesses the power to affect meaningful change, not necessarily by becoming saints or Nobel laureates, but by embarking on a personal journey of healing, self-discovery, and service.

When tragedy struck author Heidi Johnson's life she had no idea how she would survive the pain. Her life took her on the healing journey of service where she encountered stories of ordinary people who, despite facing their own adversities, have managed to make extraordinary contributions to society. They remind us that the capacity to serve others lies within all of us, waiting to be discovered and harnessed for the greater good. By tapping into our unique gifts and channeling them towards helping others, we can follow in the footsteps of these unsung heroes who dedicate their lives to serving humanity.

Through acts of service, both big and small, we not only uplift those around us but also find fulfillment and purpose in our own lives. By fostering connections, supporting one another, and embracing a mindset of giving, we can navigate through life's challenges and setbacks with resilience and grace. Ultimately, by choosing kindness, empathy, and service, we can collectively create a ripple effect of positive change that reverberates across communities, leaving behind a legacy of compassion and hope for generations to come.

Together, we can make the world a better place, one small act of kindness at a time. Ready to join the movement? Grab your copy, and let's start changing lives for good, including yours.

CHAPTER ONE

Creating Change

"No matter what you did, no matter who you are, no matter where you've come from, you can always change, become a better version of yourself."
—Madonna

If you could change the world, would you? What would you change? Eliminate war, hunger, illness, suffering? Of course, we all would if we could, but how? How could I change the world? The thought is so big and overwhelming that it shuts us down. What could I possibly do? I am just one person. What if I told you that you have the power to change the world, to make people's lives better and improve your own in the process? Would you want to try? My hope is that your answer will be yes.

Change for Good is about the journey that each of us must walk in our own unique way. It is our life's mission to find out why we are here. What do we care about and how do we want to make our world better? It is living a legacy life and not a resume one. Do you want to be remembered for your career or how you made others feel? What values do you have that you want to live out? We have many opportunities to make a difference with our time and our lives.

To this day, I still have people that tell me how much my mother's funeral impacted their life. People left her service inspired by how she lived. She made everyone in her presence feel valued and heard. My mom made her family, her friends and her community her priority. Her time was spent living those values. Although my mom's life ended at the age of 60, she made a significant impact on the world through all of the lives she touched. Isn't that how we all want to be remembered—and, more importantly, how we all want to live?

The choice is ours alone. We decide how we use our time and choose to live our lives. People like to talk about balance. I truly do not care for that word at all. Life is not about balance. It is about choices. It is that simple. Yet, somehow after we get our work done, our laundry, make dinner, flip through our social media and realize that we put aside all of the things that really matter. It's time that we change that script. It is time that we make choices that give us more joy, more gratitude, purpose, connection and physical and mental health benefits that we receive when we give.

This is not a manual on how to become a saint, a Nobel prize winner or even more like Mother Teresa. This is a journey towards healing, goodness and self-empowerment. Your journey to discover your gifts and find the best way to use them to help yourself and the world. This is a journey to change for good.

The world is a scary place. We can choose to be afraid of what we see, or we can choose to see the beauty, grace and kindness that we do not see on the nightly news. It is all around us. Remarkable humans doing work every day to create a better world. When you think of remarkable humans, people like Mother Teresa, the Dalai Lama, Gandhi, and Malala come to mind. What do all of those amazing humans have in common? They serve others. They use their gifts to help others.

With over eight billion people on this planet, there are way more than only four "good ones". The reality is that most of us are good. We are no different than Mother Teresa, Malala, Gandhi or the Dalai Lama. The only difference is that we have not yet discovered our gifts and how to put them to work. Pablo Picasso said, "*The meaning of life is to find your gift. The purpose of life is to give it away."* He was correct. We all have incredible gifts, but we haven't discovered them or found the best way to use them. Mother Teresa did, and you will too!

The people you will meet in this book are modern-day heroes who create businesses designed to help people. What sets these heroes apart from us mere mortals is that they used their pain as fuel for good by discovering their gifts and putting them to use. The sad reality is that you have never heard of any of them. Yet, these people are changing the world for the better every day.

Everyone on this planet is faced with challenges, loss and adversity at some point in their lives. We all get handed a bad hand at least once. It isn't the adversity but what they did with that pain and their challenges that set them apart. These heroes turned pain into purpose. Their lives are manuals on how to live an authentic, glorious, joyful and purposeful experience with your limited time here on earth. The reality is that you have the same choices. It is my hope that by meeting these heroes and seeing the similar patterns that we all face, we can learn valuable lessons from their stories that help us shape our futures.

Life on earth has become messy. We are seeing the erosion of the nuclear family. When families fall apart, so do the people inside of them. We see mental health challenges in our young students like never before. People feel lonely, isolated, disconnected, depressed and overwhelmed. We are seeing people who no longer have the safety and support of family, turning away from religion, community and connection. We are digitally connected like never before, but we are connected but not connected. This disconnection has led us down a dark, lonely and isolating path.

There is hope in the most basic, simple and primitive solution, and that is simply taking care of one another. It is what we, as humans, have done since the dawn of time. Somehow along the way, we got lost and became more worried about ourselves than our neighbors, our communities, our country and our world. There is not one "silver bullet" that cures all our challenges, helps us overcome insurmountable obstacles, makes us physically healthier and supports our mental health. The closest thing we have to that "silver bullet" is service.

We have the ability to help one another in little and big ways and, in the process, heal and help ourselves. How do I know this? Because I have walked this journey. When tragedy struck my family over twenty years ago and turned my world upside down, I was shattered. The process of digging out from that loss felt insurmountable. I was overwhelmed, lost in grief and saw no clear path forward. Slowly, the signs began to present themselves, the obstacles became hurdles to leap over, and my confidence grew stronger with each challenge overcome. My gifts became clearer. Grace, gratitude and love all became a life of purpose through service. Service to others healed me in remarkable ways. The butterfly came out of the cocoon and yours will too. The process of metamorphosis is one we all must endure to survive and ultimately thrive. Each journey is unique. We all have pain on our journeys, but how we evolve from that pain to help others on their journeys is what makes the process of healing and change remarkable.

For the past twenty years, service has healed me, connected and lifted me. I am not alone in this experience. I am not a missionary, a Peace Corps member or a saint—not even close. I have been described by some as the combination of a Catholic schoolgirl meets a salty sailor. There is no halo here. This is not a story of redemption but of evolution. I have but one life to live, and my story is not a model of purity, piousness or sainthood. Rather, it is a story of evolution, of clarity, of becoming, of service, and ultimately, a story of faith. It's about my journey of believing in God, in myself and in the service of others as the ultimate change for good.

Growing Up

I spent a lifetime in Catholic school, or at least what felt like a lifetime. Themes of service, giving and kindness were all around. Those were things for other people like nuns, priests and saints and definitely not for me. I spent more time in the principal's office than I did doing good deeds. In looking back at my somewhat mischievous behavior, I like to think of them as early signs of leadership.

I came from a large Irish Catholic family where we went to church, had family dinners every Sunday and took care of one another. It was a simple time growing up in the 1970s, where family was front and center, regardless of what it looked like. Every single television show was about family: *The Brady Bunch, The Waltons, Little House on the Prairie, Good Times,* and *All in the Family.* Everyone had one, and everyone had a job or responsibility in their and to their family. All of my friends had chores. We couldn't go out and play until our chores were done. Our parents didn't do things for us, we had to do them for ourselves. First and foremost, we had to take care of the team. It was "we" before me. "Me" was not a word often heard.

As a result, we became independent, scrappy and pretty good problem solvers. What we didn't realize then was that we were also builders. What were we building, riding our bikes and hanging out with neighborhood kids? We were building community infrastructure. We were creating relationships, connections and ways of working together to solve problems. Those skills are exactly what each of us needs to return to in our change for good.

Our teamwork skills all began within our families. My dad was one of seven where the team was everything. My mom was from the Midwest. She was the baby of four raised by her widowed mother and grandmother. Neither of my parents talked of "me". Everything we did was for the we, the family, the friends, the neighbors and the community. Mothers watched each other's children, fathers helped each other with yard work and we helped our friends fix their bikes. That is just what we did. When times were challenging, my fun-loving, joyful mother would say, *"Life is tough. Toughen up!"* She was right. Life is tough and can be very hard at times. What I didn't realize then but do now is that the "we" is what pulls us through.

Somewhere along the way, collectively, our society lost sight of that and became much more focused on ourselves. It was a slow erosion, like having sand in your hands that just slipped away. You are not exactly sure how it happened, but one grain at a time slipped away and now your hand is empty. That is what happens when we only focus on ourselves, the hand is empty and so is the self. More than that, the community also breaks, and with it, its infrastructure.

We can't be team players every second of the day. We all have seasons of our lives that are more self-centered than others. None of us are saints or are perfect, we are human. I have had a huge portion of my life that was very self-centered. Some would perhaps say, all of it. Going off to college at University of Arizona was definitely all about me. As a college student, my main focus was my pack of friends, not necessarily my community. It was a season all about me.

When my parents had financial challenges in the late 1980s, I came home from college. I got a job and found a way to work. Survival and putting myself through school was my top priority. When I transferred to USC without a way to pay for school, it was an extremely challenging time. I felt alone, isolated and stuck. My friends didn't have the financial challenges that I faced and rather than having fun like most of them, I worked a lot! Those challenges ultimately became a gift, as all roadblocks do. Hard work got me to the finish line of graduation with a resume filled with sales skills. Those skills led me to jobs and ultimately, to a successful career in the software business.

Starting again

Once the obstacles were conquered, life became blissful again. I married my high school sweetheart, we bought a house and had three beautiful sons. I was living the dream, and life was good. A few short years later, when tragedy struck, all of that changed. My life, my career in the software business and everything took a dramatic and profound shift. That phone call in the middle of the night that everyone warns you about, actually came. With that call came an enormous loss, unbelievable grief for so many, and ultimately, the tectonic shift that would change my life forever and for good.

A year later, when a group of friends and I co-founded a nonprofit 501c3 organization, healing began to happen. This shift from focusing on my pain to the pain of others, although not intentional, was the beginning of healing, growing and becoming. This was not my plan, none of it was. Looking in the rearview mirror I now see so clearly what I did not see before. I see in my crystal clear hindsight that this happened for me and not to me. When life handed me this card, I did not know how to play it. I did not know how this bad hand would change my life for good.

All I knew at the time was that my beautiful life was in shambles, but what I learned is that it all begins with loss. There is no forest without a fire, and there is no new city without an earthquake. Loss hits us like a landslide and it all just comes down and we are buried not sure which way is up. Little by little, we begin to dig, and with each shovel towards the light, we become stronger in our belief that we will get out from under. Our resilience and strength come from overcoming the challenges. Our lives can radically shift for the better once we come through the other side. This is how we begin to change for good.

Charity Matters

Life on the other side was good. Radically different but good. It was as if I was wearing dark glasses my entire life until digging out of the landslide. I could finally see clearly what mattered, what was important and how to use my time. The change for good was slow, but it happened. When it does, like all good things, you want more.

This was a new kind of more. I wanted that amazing feeling that you get when you help someone—more connection, more gratitude, more joy, and more life stories! I went in pursuit of changing for good after co-founding a nonprofit. After running the organization, I wanted to learn more about others who had done this work. The 1.6 million crazy humans who started a business that relies on the kindness of others to solve some of humanity's biggest problems. Who were these crazy people? I knew my crazy story, but what was theirs? Who were these entrepreneurs, modern-day heroes and crazy people who did this work?

At the time, there were no TV shows, magazines or books about nonprofit heroes. I went on my own mission to find these amazing humans—everyday people who change their lives to serve others. I wanted to find my tribe, understand them, learn from them and hear their stories. How was it possible that the world didn't know some of the best people on earth? I became an archeologist in search of these people and uncovering their stories.

Like all things, it started with a dream. An actual dream. I am one of those people that sleeps through everything. Not my proudest trait because I am such a sound sleeper that I often don't hear my children crying. Who does that? My point is that I also rarely dream or rarely remember dreams. In 2009, when I had a dream so vivid and real that it woke me up, I had to write it down. The dream was that I had a television show about nonprofit founders.

The next morning, I called my old neighbor, David, who had written for television and asked him how to write a television show. David told me to go to the WGA, Writers Guild of America, to register my treatment, and I did. Once I wrote the television show, I thought, maybe I should do some more research and begin finding these people. I figured it could take some time for my show, so in the meantime, I would start one of these new things called a blog.

Charity Matters was born, and I went in search of this tribe of extraordinary individuals who give their lives to serve. Since that time, I have interviewed hundreds of nonprofit founders and have had the privilege of learning from their journeys and sharing their stories through our blog and podcast. These modern-day heroes have renewed my hope in humanity. They are the true inspiration for this book and the life lessons they have shared have recommitted me to my belief that when we help one another, we heal one another. When we heal, we change for good.

As a storyteller, all I can do is listen to the wisdom of these people's journeys and learn from their experiences, suffering and loss. By sharing their stories of courage, compassion and kindness, we can use their loss to make another's life better. We can reflect on our challenges and use these stories as road maps to navigate our setbacks as we strive to change for good. Charity Matters and storytelling from my heroes continues to be my passion. My purpose is to be a messenger of service by sharing these inspirational stories.

TACSC

A decade ago, when I was approached to take over a nonprofit whose founder was not in great health. The organization was called TACSC, pronounced task, and it stands for The Association of Catholic Student Councils. Student Council, what did I know about that? Nothing! Catholic? No way! To be honest, my three boys were in middle school at the time, and I didn't understand what it was that this organization with a really bad name did. I was definitely not taking on this dusty, musty church lady nonprofit. I had other great job offers from "sexier" organizations and this was not for me.

Besides, with the nonprofit organization we had started a few years before, it felt like we had built a new house. A new logo, new business and our cause were so impactful and meaningful. Now, I was being asked to remodel a dusty old nonprofit. For anyone who has ever remodeled versus built, you know it is so much harder to remodel. When you remodel you have to keep the bones intact, the soul, the character and yet gut the insides. This was the main challenge with TACSC or The Association of Catholic Student Councils, besides its name. Remodeling an old nonprofit.

However, the more I began looking into what they were teaching these young middle school students, the more intrigued I became. They were teaching students leadership skills, goal setting, communication skills, mentoring and how to serve. All of a sudden, I was hooked and thought I could turn this around. It was an organization with over 30,000 alumni and a huge beating heart. It lacked a functioning skeleton. Systems were broken or non-existent but what it did for students was transformative.

Now, a decade later, TACSC, as it's now called, has transformed my life and the thousands of children we are privileged to serve each year. It's hard to believe that in just the past decade, we have had the privilege of serving over 25,000 students. In each of them, we see the power of service to transform lives. We no longer focus on Student Council but are a Catholic youth leadership organization where all students have leadership potential. We teach college students leadership, who in turn teach high school students leadership, and the high school students teach the middle school students. Students teaching students to be the best of themselves.

Most of our students attend Catholic Schools and come from all walks of life. Sadly, as we see families come apart, faith and communities disintegrate and we see mental health challenges increase. In the past ten years, especially since COVID, I have seen an increased number of depressed middle and high school students. They show up to our programs, disconnected from one another and themselves and connected to their device alone. In four days, they are re-energized, connected, validated and transformed by the power of service. One by one, I have witnessed the power of service to connect, inspire, and guide a positive upward trajectory from being a part of service. Thousands of our students at TACSC give back by teaching what they have been taught, and the cycle of goodness continues.

For these reasons and many more, I hope this message can become not only an action plan for you but have a ripple effect in your home, neighborhood, community, and ultimately, in our world. We are all here to serve one another and to discover our gifts to do just that. It is my hope that these stories and self-reflection questions will become tools you can use to heal yourself and others in the process.

We are all on a journey to become the best versions of ourselves. To learn from our challenges, to grow from loss, to find a practice of gratitude and to know that our life has left this world just a little better because we were here. We live in a world where we feel that we have so little control and are helpless. Yet, when we smile at a stranger, offer to let someone go in front of us in line at the store or show the smallest kindness, we take that control back. We make a difference, and that ripple effect has profound positive effects. When we see the good in people, it becomes easy to motivate ourselves to be of service to them. By being of service to other people and giving them value, you not only make their lives better, but over time, you get what you give. The people you help may feel more inclined to help other people. So, together you create an upward spiral of positive energy and change that grows and becomes stronger and stronger. We create change for good.

CHAPTER TWO

We Have Problems

"I alone cannot change the world, but I can cast a stone across the water to create many ripples."
—Mother Teresa

Let's be honest—we all have problems. Some big, some little but all of us have them. Think for a moment about a few of your challenges. Taking care of an aging parent, raising a family, working and trying to juggle everything. How do we fix them? Usually not alone. Since the beginning of time, humans have helped one another. Why? Because humans are messy. We are not perfect beings and there are many problems that come with being human. In recognizing our inherent messiness, we acknowledge the need for mutual support to overcome the problems that come with our human experience. Helping with a friend's children, driving an aging parent to an appointment or reaching out to a friend for a walk who is overwhelmed. The reality is that we need one another to solve many of these. We are better together.

In ancient times, cavemen and tribes helped one another in essential ways such as creating fire, finding food and protecting one another. These challenges have endured over time, evolving alongside humanity. Today, as our world expands, so do our problems. The complexities we face as a species have expanded, presenting new dilemmas that still require the tribe to come together. In this effort to survive, sharing resources, skills and knowledge was not a choice but a necessity. Ancient man knew what modern man has often forgotten: that we all need one another.

Within our tribes, a unique system of reciprocity emerged, fostering a deep sense of communal responsibility. We understood that helping one another went beyond family ties and encompassed the entire group. Each member played a vital role in the well-being of their community. These early bonds formed the basis for the evolving social structures we still see today within thriving communities.

Today, while much has changed, the need to help one another and to create community has remained. Where nonprofits go, community and connection follow. A few years back, I was actively doing yoga pretty regularly, and I was talking to my yoga teacher about starting a nonprofit. She told me that creating community is how we heal. Words I have thought of many times over the years. Then she introduced me to her friend, Jill Eppiltio Weiss, who founded Uprising Yoga. Jill went into the juvenile hall to teach these young people how to deal with their trauma and to heal through yoga.

Jill's Story

The mission of <u>Uprising Yoga</u> is to bring trauma-informed yoga to the incarcerated and to underserved communities. Trauma-informed yoga helps people understand the impact of trauma on their entire mind and body, it helps understand the imprint left on the brain.

We have now had such growth that we are training the trainers to bring our program to social workers, probation staff and more teacher awareness. We are building sustainable business models where others can take our curriculum into their communities and use trauma-informed yoga.

In the summer of 2010, I was dating a man named Nick, now my husband, and he came home from work and was shaking and upset. I asked what was wrong, and he explained that he had just toured a youth prison camp. He described what he saw, and I asked him, "Can I teach yoga there?"

I was working at a yoga college with my friend Mary and she was trying to put a group of instructors together to teach in the juvenile hall already. Between the two of us, we tried to find a way to actually get into juvenile hall. Getting clearance to work in prisons is a big deal. For months we tried to offer our services and got nowhere. Then, in 2011, Nick and I were at a Christmas party and I was talking to a man who worked in the prison system and told him what I wanted to do. He and his colleagues all reached out and said, "When do you want to start?" So Mary, Nick and I began teaching trauma-informed yoga on Tuesday nights to the juvenile hall's most vulnerable kids—the foster care sexually trafficked minors.

Slowly, the classes began to grow and grow. We received a grant to determine how yoga was helping these kids. A friend said, "Have you thought about starting a nonprofit?" So, in 2012, we started officially. We were having a fundraiser and I called my mom to ask if she would donate. She asked what for and I told her to help the kids in juvenile hall. My mom said, "Jill, I picked you up there when you were a kid." I was speechless because I honestly did not remember that I had been in the juvenile hall that I was now teaching in. Because I didn't remember, I began to study trauma and how it affects your brain and how we heal from trauma. That is how I connected trauma and yoga.

I knew that I had gotten into trouble, and I knew that recovery and yoga had saved my life. I hadn't really been able to figure out why I was drawn to incarcerated youth until that moment. What pulled at my heart is that my mom came for me, and no one is coming for these kids.

My work matters. The ultimate gift is hearing how you changed someone's life for the better. There are so many ways, but when we receive a letter, an email or a picture from juvenile hall saying, "Thank you for caring about us." I know we are teaching life skills and that what we teach lasts a

24 | The Transformative Power of Giving As The Ultimate Cure

lifetime. I was recently asked to participate in a book about best practices for yoga in the criminal justice system. When people recognize me for my work that is touching.

We recently had a hostage/shooter situation at our local Trader Joe's, a block from our home. The day after the situation, I volunteered my services to teach trauma-informed yoga to the hostages. I felt so helpless and thought, what can one person do to offer their gifts and talents? There was so much pain and trauma in my own neighborhood. So now we come together once a week and the trauma-informed yoga has brought us all together. Yoga is healing these victims of violence and has given me an opportunity to use my gifts to let others know I care. These hostages have told me how this class has healed them.

Our impact is on many levels. It can be as small as what we do for one person with our one-on-one work or large when we do large events. We know that violence goes down significantly after we work in the prisons. Today, our work is recognized nationally and internationally. Our <u>Uprising Yoga</u> curriculum is spreading across the country because it works and people are replicating our model. That is when you know your work has an impact.

I have learned that people are good and want to keep doing good. Once the nonprofit got started, people who cared came out of the woodwork to volunteer, to help, to donate and that literally shifted my entire perception of humanity. I didn't know people had SO much good in them. I continue to believe that.

This experience made me go from suspicion and confusion to understanding why I went through my pain and how my healing process became available to others. I understood what my own healing journey meant. The yoga didn't heal just me but it also healed everyone around me. My husband Nick has been a part of this entire journey and I feel that our love is shared out into a community.

Jill's story teaches us so many lessons about creating change for good. She discovered her gift as a yoga instructor and found a way to share that gift with others. In the process, she created community, connection and healing in her work and neighborhood. Jill did all of this by using her gifts for good. It was that simple. Helping one another is what we humans have always done.

The Nonprofit

As our world and civilization grew and developed, so did our problems and our need to work together for solutions. Building better communities and societies means working together to solve the problems of humanity. Whatever the problem, working in a community is usually the solution. When we think of those solutions, we think of nonprofit organizations for building community infrastructure and solutions.

It wasn't until 1917 that the US Government created the tax-exempt status for twenty-six types of organizations. It was the tax code 501c3 that represents the public charity that created the modern-day nonprofit as we know it. This was the beginning of the modern-day nonprofit organization. The reality is that we have always helped one another, but now we have financial incentives to do good.

This sense of community, support and connection is at the core of who we are. People who help one another. The roots our country was built upon involve charity, philanthropy and volunteerism. It is at the core of what it means to be American. Our nonprofit organizations are a silent force that shapes our communities, uplifts lives and spreads hope far and wide. These organizations are the unsung heroes of our society whose impact reverberates across every section of our country. Nonprofits serve as a cross-section of all Americans and fill the gap that exists between business and government.

Did you know that there are a staggering 1.5 million nonprofit organizations in the United States alone? These are more than numbers; they represent individuals who had a dream to make life better for their communities. From fighting hunger to championing education, from protecting the environment to advocating for human rights, the nonprofit stands as a beacon of change, illuminating the path for brighter tomorrows.

It isn't just about the sheer number of nonprofits; it's about the people behind them. The driving force that propels their missions forward. Ten percent of the workforce in the United States is employed by nonprofits. That is a significant chunk of our fellow citizens dedicated to making a difference every single day. More than that, it is the lives that are transformed by these individuals and the impact made on some of our biggest problems.

The impact of nonprofits extends beyond the United States and reaches every corner of the globe. Here are a few facts about nonprofits:

- Nonprofit organizations employ 7.4% of the worldwide workforce.
- 70% of these workers are paid and 29% are volunteers.
- 5.7% of the United States GDP comes from nonprofits
- The United States annual revenue for nonprofits is a staggering $2.63 trillion dollars
- 56% of Americans donated to charity in 2021

Millions of Americans give, we are often confused between the definition of charity and philanthropy. To many of us, they are the same and yet there are nuanced differences that set these two definitions and the scope of how we give apart. Understanding the different ways our lives can impact others helps us to assess how we want to use our own lives to make a difference.

Definition of Charity and Philanthropy:

Charity has existed since the beginning of time, but the word itself brings to mind images of people with their hands outstretched, asking for money. For many of us, the word charity has a negative connotation, bringing up images of people suffering or thoughts of the poor. Others hear the word and connect it with guilt from not doing enough. It is amazing the power one simple word has to bring forth a variety of associations and thoughts.

Over a decade ago, when I named my blog Charity Matters, I heard firsthand from many friends and associates that they didn't understand what I was trying to do. My mission to help the helpers and to become a messenger that service heals was confusing to many. Then I realized that was in part because so many of us think about charity in very different ways.

Even the dictionaries' definitions are not the same. The Oxford Dictionary defines charity as, *"an organization set up to provide help and raise money for those in need."* Or as, *"the voluntary giving of help, typically in the form of money to those in need."* That is not the only definition of charity.

Merriam-Webster Dictionary defines charity as:

1. "Generosity and helpfulness especially toward the needy or suffering."
2. "An institution engaged in relief of the poor."
3. "Public provision for the relief of the needy."
4. "Benevolent goodwill towards or love of humanity."

It is that last definition that I most identify with, love of humanity. The Bible refers to charity many times. In full disclosure, I am not well versed in the Bible, but Timothy 1:5 says, *"We have pure love, when from the heart, we show genuine concern and compassion for our brothers and sisters.*" In short, if I had to pick one definition of charity, it would be the love of man or humanity.

I was often asked by friends why I didn't name my blog and podcast Philanthropy Matters. I have to confess my word association with philanthropy is a fancy word for charity. While I know this is not true, it is an assumption made by many. The Merriam-Webster Dictionary defines philanthropy as "*Goodwill to fellow members of the human race.*" As well as, "*An act or gift made for humanitarian purposes or an organization supported by funds set aside for humanitarian purposes.*"

So, what is the difference between charity and philanthropy? According to Google, "*Philanthropy is more long-term and strategic and often involves making multiple gifts to help people over a number of years. While charity is focused on providing immediate relief to people and is often driven by emotions. Philanthropy is focused on helping people and solving their problems over the long term.*" Again, loving one another as defined by short and long-term goals doesn't feel right either. Who am I to question Google?

Some organizations, like Giving Compass, define charity as a "*Natural emotional impulse to an immediate situation and giving usually occurs in the short term. Charity can take the form of monetary donations or volunteering.*" Think of how many times you have scrolled through your Facebook or social media and received a GoFundMe about someone you know who needs immediate help from an illness or injury. You don't even think, you just give because you care. It is like an automatic response. You don't look at your bank account, you just hit send.

Giving Compass defines philanthropy as, "*Addressing the root cause of social issues and requires a more strategic, long-term approach. In addition to giving money or volunteering, some philanthropists participate in advocacy work.*" Again, that links to giving and strategy, which we see so many people doing today with their resources.

When many of us think of philanthropy, we think of fancy wealthy billionaires putting their names on buildings or hosting benefits. By the way, there is absolutely nothing wrong with people who have gobs of money giving it away in any way that they see fit. Anyone who gives should be commended regardless of circumstances. A homeless person who gives change to a friend in need or a billionaire who gives millions to a cause they care about. We all do what we can with what we have. It is not my place or anyone else's to judge who gives what.

I don't think I'm alone. That is one of the reasons I am writing this book. Our brains want to label and file information, we can't help it, it is how we are wired. Just like nonprofit organizations, there are more than a few different types of helpers who commit themselves in ways little and big to change the world. When typically thinking of the helpers, we think of three or four basic labels or categories. Let's look at them in order of our perception of who we think makes the most impact.

Defining the helpers

The Philanthropist

The first category is the one we were just talking about: the philanthropists. These are people helping in a huge financial and generous way. You know Warren Buffett, Bill Gates, the Rockefellers or the Carnegies. These are people who take The Giving Pledge to give fifty percent of their wealth away before they die. They are often the same people whose names are on college buildings, who run or have foundations used to help solve problems, sometimes even their own tax problems. These people are often incredibly successful in business and have natural problem-solving skills. Later in their lives, when they have the resources of time and money, they turn their skills towards taking on some of life's challenging problems. They are choosing to use their resources and gifts to create a positive impact. One of those philanthropists is a wonderful man named Larry Gilson.

Larry's Story

Larry Gilson is a kind, charming, intelligent communicator and a man who built an incredible career and business. After a brilliant career in private equity and even a stint in Jimmy Carter's White House, Larry was ready for a new challenge. He is a natural problem solver and a big thinker. After he sold his business, he now had some time and additional resources to take on some of life's biggest challenges, both locally and abroad. Larry went looking for an organization that could give him choices for his resources and real impact on his investment. Just as he had done in his career with private equity where he invested in people to provide an impact.

Larry told me, "*I thought with all of the philanthropic activity that takes place in the United States, there will be lots of resources available that we could tap into that were identifying compelling, giving opportunities in a professional confidence-inspiring way. I spent almost a year looking for this hypothetical resource. I kept looking because I couldn't believe I wasn't finding it. But my expectations were high because I was looking for something with the same lens as the investment decision-making tools that my firm had built over the span of decades. When I wasn't finding what I was looking for, I started asking friends who were in a similar situation. They had a similar lament about their own experience and asked me, 'Can we ride your coattails and get the benefit of their research?' I said, 'Okay, maybe I should do something more ambitious.' And that became the genesis of Focusing Philanthropy.*"

Larry told me, "*For the past 11 years we've been a version of what it was I was looking for. We now have a team of eight people who do the research, the exploration of potential giving opportunities, the ongoing monitoring, the crafting of giving appeals and accurate and timely reporting. What we do for our own family, we now do for about 450 other families around the world with most of them in the United States.*"

Today Focusing Philanthropy has made a significant impact in a very intentional way. They split their resources between the United States and international causes. Larry shared one example of their impact when he said, "*We have only 14 or 15 nonprofits in our roster at any one time. About half of our nonprofits are domestic and half are international. One international partner is called One Acre Fund. Half of the world's extremely poor people have something in common aside from poverty, and that is they're farmers. They're planting their crops, they're harvesting what they plant and their family is mainly eating everything that they harvest. So, they're really not even creating a surplus that allows them to sell into the market and generate cash profits.*

When we started with them, in 2012, they were working with about 40,000 farmers in Western Kenya and they had jumped the border into Rwanda and Burundi. Now, 11 years later, we've been a catalytic partner for all the intervening period, they're now working in nine countries, working with one and a half million farm families, where the average farmer has six relatives that they support. They're doing the hard work and they're learning the skills. We're giving them the tools, the support and the network of resources that enable them to be successful. You do the math—that's 9 million people who are permanently out of starvation and poverty as a result of this impact.

We start with the observation that Americans are the most generous people in the world philanthropically. Our experience is that philanthropic activity hasn't always been the most fulfilling, rewarding or confidence-inspiring. People have the impulse to be generous, but they also want to be confident that what they're contributing actually makes a difference.

The more people give, I think the more they have a series of questions that are in their heads. But I think they want to know, if I give dollars to such and such an organization, can I be confident that it'll actually be used in the way that I intended that they promise? Will I get good feedback on what's actually happened? Will more dollars just result in more activity, but not necessarily a more meaningful impact? How do I choose among organizations that are all announcing themselves as being active in a particular space?

These are challenging questions. The answers take quite a bit of time and effort to come up with, and most people are busy doing other things. We're trying to fill that gap to answer those questions. We want to give people the confidence to make informed choices, and to have the sense of satisfaction that comes from getting good feedback. That's the niche that we're trying to fill."

Larry's story reminds us of what one person can do to make a huge impact on the world. He chooses to use his resources to change for good for people all over the world. Remarkable people like Larry, who care, can make incredible change possible. The philanthropists are smart, generous, and usually, very strategic about their donations. They give significantly, and as a result, their impact is equally significant. These individuals create major change and should be revered for their contributions to society.

The Humanitarian

The second way we categorize the helpers of the world is the humanitarian. The humanitarian is often found in a developing nation, working for the Peace Corps or on the streets with the homeless. They are the real superstars of our world often found in National Geographic magazine, living in some of the most repressed areas of the globe. We look at them as outliers or slightly crazed and yet we respect them. These people are happy, they are incredibly hard workers, and they sacrifice comforts to serve others. They are the frontline workers at some of life's most difficult places and work endlessly to relieve human suffering.

Kurt's Story

One of those humanitarians is Kurt Kandler, the founder of Bridge 410. I met Kurt shortly after he had written his first book. His nonprofit is redefining the war on poverty in Kenya, Uganda, Haiti and Guatemala. He told me his amazing story of going from an Atlanta suburban dad to a humanitarian.

Our kids were going to a small private school in Atlanta. They were presented with this opportunity in Uganda. The kids in the school were sending shoeboxes full of toys and school supplies. A family went over there to take these school boxes to Uganda. They came back and I was looking at pictures of their trip.

I came across a photo of a school building that was made out of mud, sticks, cow dung and dirt floors. Kids sat on rocks and there were no teachers. And I just was fascinated by this idea that they had to repack the walls of this school building every time it rained. It just captured me and captured my heart. I decided what I'm going to do is I'm going to go over there and I'm going to go build them a brick building.

We went over there to build this brick building school block. And we did that We had to raise money for a school building, for a water project, textbooks and all of that. In my view, it wasn't solving a problem.

I just was captured by the real problems that contributed to extreme poverty. It's my first exposure to extreme poverty. I certainly had more questions than answers, but I came back and became a bit of a student and read a lot about it. I found very early on that there was a lot written about the problem and why it existed.

I really felt compelled and I had an idea of how to go execute on that. Which is really crazy, because it is a big, complicated problem—a huge problem. I felt like what if we could focus on a place? Really go deep into that place for an extended period of time? Could we move the needle in that place and really begin to solve this poverty problem for that place?

"When we think about impact, our ultimate goal with a community is to work ourselves out of a job as quickly as we can. This is a very long-term walk that we walk with the community. I was in a community last week, which will be our 13th graduating community. We've been walking with them for 12 to 13 years. It's been a long time. What does it mean to graduate? In order to graduate, we have to reach certain outcomes. With the leaders in the community, we outline outcomes that they want to see happen. Before we begin, we decide that we will finish with water after we finish with education. When we finish with economic empowerment, what are the outcomes we're looking for? What I want to know: Is this program that we're running in this community going to achieve the outcome that the leaders of the community set forth?

If you think about household income, an outcome for us is we want to move people from whatever they're making today, call it sub $2 a day to $12 per day. They have choices that they can make about their quality of life. We set up outcomes. As we start achieving those outcomes, and we get to maybe 80% of the outcomes achieved, we'll start teeing up and introducing the idea of graduation to the leaders. Within a year or two, they will end up graduating and have a huge celebration in the community.

A huge celebration at the end of this year with that community and partners and donors will come and the whole community will come out. We'll celebrate not what we did—we're gonna celebrate what the community has done on their own because we don't measure our success by what we do. We measure our success by what the community does on its own. And when they do that, it is amazing to see people have this aha moment that says we will never go back to being poor again.

Kurt's passion for making a difference inspires us all to think about how we are living our values and beliefs. He is a role model as a doer and a believer in good. While most Americans are kind and generous, the majority of us are not going to sell our home, move to a third-world country and dedicate our lives to helping others. The humanitarians are the Marines of the world, they go in first, they do very hard work and they are boots on the ground. Like the philanthropist, they are a unique and rare species. These are people who face life's most daunting challenges by walking alongside those they serve, often in difficult conditions. Their joy, passion and gratitude is palpable and their lives are ones of deep purpose and meaning.

The Volunteer

The third category of helpers is the largest group and applies to most of us. This category includes all the parents who work in classrooms or are involved in their child's Boy Scouts or Girl Scouts, the volunteers at the local church or maybe even that guy who runs the 10k for charity. In other words, most of us.

Here are a few fun facts about volunteers:

- According to the latest US Census Bureau, 51% of Americans aged 16 and over helped their neighbors at the height of the pandemic. That is over 124.7 million people who helped one another informally.
- 23% of that same group, or 60.7 million people, formally volunteered with an organization during that same time. One in four Americans volunteer, which is equal to 4.1 billion hours or $122.9 billion dollars

- Over one billion people formally volunteer worldwide

Since the pandemic, 75% of Americans think volunteering is more important than ever.

These volunteers, like Jill, Larry and Kurt, are the lifeline for thousands of charities and nonprofits that couldn't survive without them and their dedication. It doesn't matter whether you are a philanthropist, a humanitarian or a volunteer, each person plays a vital role in using their life to make others better. These combined efforts touch lives, restore hope and realize dreams because of the tireless efforts of these unsung heroes who change our world.

Reflection

1. Reflect on your own volunteer experiences and journal what experiences brought you joy and why.
2. Can you think of anyone you know who actively volunteers? What traits do you see in those people that inspire you?
3. What areas are you interested in? Education, Health, Military, Humanitarian, animals, the environment? You can pick more than one.
4. Think about the larger category and then begin to dig deeper. For example: If Health is the larger category. Think about what specific health category that you are interested in? An example would be heart health.
5. Next, ask yourself **why** you are interested in organizations that help people with heart health, for example.
6. Clearly state your why.

Example: I am interested in exploring people becoming heart-healthy because my family has a long history of heart disease.

I am interested in exploring_____because of _____.

CHAPTER THREE

The Benefits of Giving

"Those who are happiest are those who do the most for others." —Booker T. Washington

Why do all these people do all this good? Believe it or not, giving does more good than just helping someone—we actually help ourselves in life-changing ways. I never truly understood the profound impact of serving others until it healed me in unimaginable ways from loss. The journey opened my eyes to a world that extended far beyond simple acts of giving. When we give, the benefits are profound.

Have you ever found yourself relying on the help of a stranger before? I remember years ago, before there were cell phones, I was in a car accident. I had just bought my first car after graduating from college, the paper plates were still on it, when I made a blind left and totaled the car. I was 23 years old. Alone, scared on a dark rainy night, I went up to a stranger's house in a nice neighborhood in LA and knocked on the door. When the woman answered, I began to cry, telling her I had been in an accident. She called her husband and they kindly invited me in to use their phone. The couple asked me to stay inside with them and join them for dinner.

I will never forget that couple's kindness. A few days later, with my new loaner, I went by with flowers and a note. Again, they answered the door and told me how glad they were that I was ok. They told me that they were happy to help. It was their pleasure and their hope that if it was their daughter, someone would have done the same.

Reflecting on that story from long ago, I remember the joy the couple had when I came by to thank them. Their joy stayed with me as a reminder of how we should all be. It's so easy to ignore someone, yet they didn't. It turns out that those lovely people were wise. People who help one receive incredible benefits from giving.

Physical Health

It may seem surprising, but serving others can have significant benefits for your physical health. When you engage in acts of service, your body responds in remarkable ways!

Serving others reduces our stress levels and acts as a natural stress reliever. By focusing on someone else's needs, it shifts your attention away from your own. That diversion can significantly lower stress levels and create a sense of calm.

In turn, that calm can have profound effects on our improved physical health.

Studies have shown that individuals who regularly engage in acts of service tend to have better overall physical health. Acts of kindness have been linked to lower blood pressure, reduced risk of heart disease and even a strengthened immune system. The positive emotions associated with helping others can have a direct impact on your body's well-being.

Believe it or not, serving others may even help you to live longer! A 2012 study by the University of Michigan determined that older people who volunteer with regularity tend to live longer than those who don't, but only if your intentions are altruistic. The same study said, "*Those who volunteered for self-oriented reasons had a mortality risk similar to nonvolunteers.*" Translation is that you must truly want to help others to feel better. The sense of purpose and fulfillment that comes from helping others may contribute to a healthier, more resilient body.

Last year, the Cleveland Clinic published an article entitled, "Why Giving is Good for Your Health." In this article, psychologist Susan Albers, PsyD, describes the chemical reaction that takes place every time you do something nice. The serotonin regulates your mood, dopamine for a sense of pleasure and oxytocin a positive sense of connection with others. Dr. Albers said, "Giving can stimulate the brain's mesolimbic pathway and release endorphins that boost self-esteem, combat depression, and reduce levels of the stress hormone cortisol, as well as lowering blood pressure and protecting your heart."

Mental Health

In addition to the physical advantages that serving others has, there is also a profound impact on your mental well-being. The act of giving can more than lift your spirits and boost your mood, it can provide a sense of fulfillment that few other activities can match. A report by Angela Thoreson on the Mayo Clinic website said that, *"Volunteering improves the physical and mental health of adults over 60 and lowers the rates of depression and anxiety for those over 65."*

One of the most immediate benefits of serving others is the sense of happiness it brings. Whether you're helping a stranger in need or volunteering for a cause you care about, the act of giving can evoke feelings of joy and contentment. In a study published in 2020 in the *Journal of Happiness Studies,* researchers examined data from nearly 70,000 research participants in the United Kingdom. These participants received surveys about their volunteering habits and mental health from 1996 to 2014. Those who volunteered at least once a month reported better mental health than participants who volunteered infrequently or not at all.

Isolation and loneliness are sadly becoming more prevalent. Serving others can combat those feelings. By connecting with those in need, you begin to form meaningful relationships. Those relationships create a sense of connection and belonging that can fight off feelings of isolation and replace them with feelings of connection.

Service is not only fighting off depression and loneliness, but it is building resilience in the face of adversity. With the hundreds of nonprofit founders I have interviewed in the past decade, this resilience is a common thread. I experienced this myself when we started the nonprofit The Spiritual Care Guild. By focusing on the mission at hand, others whose problems seem infinitely bigger than your own, you gain new insight and perspective into your own problems. The result is a deep sense of inner strength that allows you to weather life's storms with grace and resilience.

I knew service had helped me overcome adversity and that it helped me get out of my head during a dark period. When my 13-year-old son was not immediately accepted into a high school he wanted to attend, he went into a funk. It wasn't a depression, but it was a huge hormonal pity party. Nothing we could do seemed to snap him out of it. He had always been an upbeat person, so we were now concerned parents as his mental health deteriorated.

At the time, I was involved in a Cristo Rey School, in Watts, an area of South Central Los Angeles, called Verbum Dei. The school was located next to the housing projects called Nickerson Gardens, where the residents lived in poverty. According to the LAPD, there were more firearms in those projects than LAPD possessed. There was a small nonprofit called Urban Compass that was located on Verbum Dei's gated and safe campus. After school, the young children who lived in the projects came next door to the high school campus to be tutored, do their homework and be kept safe until their parents were home from work. I inquired if there might be a summer program that my 13-year-old son could help out with. The answer was, "Yes! We would love to have him."

I drove Hunter 40 minutes each way down to Watts for his summer of sadness. About a week after volunteering, the Executive Director, Theresa, asked me, "Can Hunter help me walk the kids home into the projects at night?" I said, "Of course!" When I picked Hunter up that first night after walking into Nickerson Gardens, I asked him how his day was. He said, "Mom, when I walked one of the boys home, who was maybe 6 or 7, he clung to my leg and begged me to stay. Mom, he told me, 'Please, Mr. Hunter, please don't make me go home'." Hunter said he was so confused and couldn't understand why a little boy wouldn't want to go home. I asked Hunter, "What did you tell him?" Hunter replied, "I got down on my knee and looked him in the eye and told him if he worked really hard at school then one day he could go to Verbum Dei. I would come every day after school until he did."

I was touched by how much this little boy meant to Hunter, but I said, "You can't make promises that you can't keep." Hunter replied, "Oh, I intend to keep it." And he did. I drove Hunter every day that summer until he eventually got into his beloved high school. When Hunter finally had what he wanted, going to this high school in LA, I thought his promise was behind him. Instead, it made him even more committed to this program and this little boy. Hunter's summer sadness was long gone. In its place was a sense of gratitude for his home, his life, his family and a renewed sense of purpose and commitment.

I drove Hunter to Watts every day for a year until he got his driver's license. Once he had his license, he drove himself for all four years of high school, keeping his word, his mental health, his confidence and his growing sense of purpose.

Social Benefits

My son's story turned around his mental health, but it also had a positive impact on the communities and relationships around him. The act of giving can strengthen bonds, foster a sense of unity and create a ripple effect of kindness that extends far beyond the act of volunteering.

When we serve, we have an opportunity to connect with people from all walks of life. Those bonds, just like in the story above, help to build empathy and understanding. By stepping outside of our comfort zones and engaging with diverse communities, you gain valuable insights into the lives and experiences of others, which fosters a greater sense of compassion and empathy. That circle of kindness grows, inspires others to follow and creates a ripple effect that spreads far and wide.

Career Benefits

Who knew that service is also good for our careers? Serving others can have a positive impact on our professional lives. Employers increasingly value candidates who demonstrate a commitment to serving others and their skill sets that come as a result of their service. Employers see in those who volunteer enhanced leadership skills, such as communication, problem-solving and empathy. Volunteering also expands your professional and social network by opening new doors and opportunities. By being involved in community events, you have an opportunity to meet a diverse range of people to offer advice, mentorship or career guidance.

Studies have shown that employees who engage in corporate volunteering programs or participate in workplace service initiatives report higher levels of job satisfaction and morale. A recent study by Benevity, a company that provides charitable donation management, found a strong link between employees that engaged in charitable giving, volunteering and other positive actions had a higher level of job retention. They also discovered there was a 52% lower turnover rate among new employees who participated in purpose programs. The sense of purpose and fulfillment that comes from serving others can translate into greater satisfaction and engagement in your professional life.

A Greater Purpose

As if physical health, mental health, social and career benefits are not enough—wait, there is still another reward, and that is having a purpose greater than yourself! It is perhaps the most significant benefit of serving others. Serving others can provide a profound sense of meaning that enriches every aspect of your life. When you commit yourself to making a difference in the lives of others, you tap into a source of fulfillment that transcends material success and personal gain. Knowing that you've made a positive impact on someone else's life, no matter how small, can fill you with a sense of purpose that money or success can not provide.

This purpose allows you to live in alignment with your core values and beliefs. When you prioritize kindness, compassion and generosity, you create a life that reflects your deepest principles and aspirations, leading to a greater sense of authenticity and fulfillment.

More than that, serving others allows you to leave a lasting legacy that extends far beyond your own lifetime. The impact of your acts of kindness can ripple through generations, inspiring others to follow in your footsteps and continue the cycle of giving for years to come. The benefits of serving others are multifaceted: physical, mental, social, career and having a greater purpose. By embracing a lifestyle of kindness and generosity, you not only enrich the lives of those around you but also experience a profound transformation within yourself. Let's embark on this journey together, one small act of kindness at a time, and discover the incredible power giving back has to transform our lives.

Reflection

1. Think of a time you helped someone. How did you feel after?
2. How did you feel when you were volunteering? Connected, happy, engaged, grateful? List some adjectives to describe your experiences

3. Are these feelings you would rate as positive? Are these feelings you would like to have more of in your life?
4. When you think of the benefits of giving: Mental health, physical health, career, social benefits and a greater sense of purpose. Which or all of these are important to you?
5. Rank the benefits from 1 to 5, with one being the most important. For example: mental health =1; career health=5; sense of purpose=3.
6. Think about how you can achieve more of your top benefits.

CHAPTER FOUR

It All Starts with Loss

*"Things we lose have a way of coming back to us in the end,
if not always in the way we expect."*
—J.K. Rowling, *Harry Potter and the Order of the Phoenix*

The Call

It's that phone call in the middle of the night—the one you are always warned about. It was 4:30 am on November 9th, 2002. My husband wakes from his sleep to find the hotel room phone. My younger sister Erin is on the other end, frantically telling him there has been a car accident in Mexico. People are dead, the US consulate had just called her with the news. Groggy and confused, he wakes me up. Neither of us is processing the call. Then my sister calls back, and she repeats that my parents and their friends were hit by a bus while on vacation in Puerto Vallarta, and three people are dead... One of the dead is my 60-year-old mom. My dad is fighting for his life.

A blood-curdling scream hurls from me, sounding like a dying animal. It feels like a piece of my soul is being torn from my body. A pain so deep, a shock so unfathomable, this has to be a mistake. This can't be real. No! No, this isn't happening. Tears, gasping for breath, the pain... My parents were in Mexico with their best friends, four couples celebrating my dad's birthday. This isn't happening, it can't be. I just said goodbye to my mom on Thursday. I was just hugging her, telling her I loved her and to have a great trip. No!

I know this must be a mistake. This isn't real. Just a few hours ago we were celebrating my husband Ron's birthday with two other couples in Ojai, having the greatest day. My dad and Ron share a birthday on November 8th. While we were with our friends away for the weekend, my parents were doing the same with their friends. Now, my mother is dead, two of my parents' friends are dead, and my dad is in a coma, fighting for his life. None of this seemed real.

In these moments of shock, something happens where your brain shuts down. The information can not be processed. Your brain can not take in all of the information and it is as if everything goes into slow motion. The reel of life needs to be played at an extra slow speed in order to process. Decisions and actions feel like molasses. Action seems to keep the processing of pain away. It is what many might call an out-of-body experience. You detach from yourself in a robotic way because you know somehow this is just a bad dream.

We called the hospital in Puerto Vallarta, where the doctor confirmed he had my father in critical condition, along with one of my dad's friends, also in bad shape. My dad had a broken back, a broken femur, all his ribs broken, a collapsed lung, and he wasn't conscious. There was only one respirator and my dad didn't have it. We asked if they had my mom, in case it was a mistake and maybe she was at another hospital. That must be it. The doctor said they had all of the survivors but did not have Judie McNiff. *Where are you, Mom? Where did you go? I'm sure you are just lost and this is a horrible mistake.*

In a daze, we gathered our things, told our friends the news and left Ojai in the opposite mood we had arrived. Heading home to LA, we called my youngest sister back, who said she was going to Mexico that afternoon. Ron agreed he would go with her. I remember getting off that call and asking Ron, "I need you to do something for me. Promise me you will ID mom and you won't let Erin see her in the morgue.

Promise me, please. Whatever you do, please don't leave Mom in Mexico, bring her home." He promised.

Ron adored my mother, and she adored him. He had ridden his bike to my house every day after school since he was 15 years old and finally, when he had his driver's license at 16, it was my mom that said, "Heidi, you should go out with him. He is such a nice boy." We always joked that if Ron and I were ever to break up, my mom would keep him. We dated for seven years before getting married. After 11 years of marriage and almost twenty years together, Ron was the son my mom never had.

Landslide

Six weeks before this fateful day, my parents decided to update their will. My mother asked Ron to be the Executor of my parent's estate. She trusted him completely, and now, he was on his way to get her body and bring my dad home. This just didn't seem real. We called Ron's parents on the two-hour drive down the coast. Ron told them the news and asked them to get him on the flight to Mexico, as Fleetwood Mac' song "Landslide"[1] played in the background...

Driving down the 101 and looking at the ocean to my right and the hills that slide down every year onto the highway to my left, I heard the words over and over, "When the landslide takes you down." It was a landslide, and I was being taken down. Tears poured down my face. Everything that I knew was falling out underneath me. I was adrift. The song continued, "Can I sail through the changin' ocean tides?" How would I survive without my mom, my first love, my anchor, my joy and the person who made everything ok? The child within my heart was instinctually terrified of life without my mom.

---

[1] Fleetwood Mac (1975). Landslide [Song]. On *Fleetwood Mac*. Reprise Records. Copyrighted by Kobalt Music Pub America I o/b/o Welsh Witch Music

"Can I handle the seasons of my life?" What did that mean? Then, Ron asked me about how we were going to tell our boys about losing their beloved grandmother. Instantly, focusing on the boys sprung me to attention and then I realized. I'm the mom and not the child. *"Well, I've been afraid of changin' Cause I built my life around you. But time makes you bolder. Even children get older and I'm gettin' older too."* How will I handle this season of my life without the person I loved so deeply, who was my anchor, my everything. Now, I needed to be a mom and share the news with our little boys, who were seven, five and one and adored their grandmother, Marmie.

My middle sister, who was pregnant and on bed rest, was due any day with my parents' only granddaughter. It was going to be my job to be the messenger. There was so much happening so quickly, and yet it also felt like it was happening in slow motion.

Telling my sister and her husband is fuzzy looking back. I think we sometimes block these painful moments from our lives as a form of self-protection. I just remember it was horrible. All of it was a living nightmare. Erin and Ron left for Mexico. I went to my parent's house, the home we had grown up in, and when I walked inside, the dam broke. My whole world had just shattered in a few hours, and it was never going to be the same again. *When the landslide takes you down...*

The following days were a blur. People showing up with food, my in-laws helping with our sons and Ron and my sister Erin in Mexico. Getting bodies out of foreign countries is notoriously not an easy process. Why I thought it was going to be easy for Ron, I will never understand. Ron had kept his promise and had identified my mom's body and kept my sister from the process. Now, he turned his attention to my dad, who was not doing well. The doctors in Mexico told Ron and Erin that my dad was not stable enough to move and that he would die if he was transported. Ron knew that he would die if he stayed there.

He was in a hospital room that looked like a cement public restroom, and he needed a ventilator. The hospital only had one ventilator, and my dad's good friend was in bad shape and needed it, too. Ron made the call—he was going to use all of his credit cards and hire a medical jet to get my dad home. He begged our other family friends to do the same, but they decided to listen to the doctors and keep their dad in Mexico a little longer.

The phone rang at my parents' house, it was a call from the US Embassy in Mexico. The woman from the Embassy was calling on behalf of Ron. She was sorry to inform me that my mother would not be going on the plane with Ron, Erin and my dad. She said, "Do you want to lose both of your parents? Your husband has no choice and he is doing the right thing. You need to know that the Embassy will get your mother home as soon as possible, but right now, we need to save your father first." Ron had told her that he had promised me and had never broken a promise. She told him that she would call his wife and explain.

Erin and Ron landed in the small jet at Burbank airport, they were taken by ambulance to Huntington Hospital, where I was waiting. I was told to bring the new copy of my dad's will and advance medical directive. I was sitting in the waiting room with the thick leather burgundy binder when the nursing staff asked for it. I went into the ICU to see my dad, and right then, he flatlined. He was dead, but they brought him back, per his directive. My dad died a second time, and again, they brought him back.

Meanwhile, the media was starting to get wind of the story of four Pasadena families in this horrible accident. The priest from one of the local parishes who knew most of the families was at the ICU desk offering last rites to my dad. The hospital's media relations person approached me and the priest and asked if I wanted to make a statement. I said, "Absolutely no media. No statement. Please keep them away." She agreed and did what I asked. It was just too much.

After my dad died twice and was resuscitated, the doctors put him in a medically induced coma to heal. My dad's six siblings came from far and wide and sat vigil every night at his bedside. He was never alone, not once. The love his siblings showed him in their vigil is something I will never forget. It inspired me, moved me and reminded me that even in loss, there is so much love. It was witnessing this love, this connection and their combined faith that gave me a life raft. My aunts and uncles gave me something to believe in, to hold onto when nothing made sense. We had what we needed to get through this—family, friends and faith.

Funerals

The first week passed, and we had the first funeral. My dad remained in a coma. Prayers, faith and hope were what we clung to each day as we sat by my dad's bedside. Despite all the loss all around us, we felt the enormous love from our friends, my parents' friends and neighbors. People came out of the woodwork to help in ways big and small. As dark as things were, we felt this incredible love and support from so many people. There was a notebook at my parents' house logging the food, the flowers, the letters, calls and errands that people were doing. My mom's good friend asked where my parents' bills were. She was going to find them and pay them or call the companies and explain. Things we couldn't even think about but needed to happen. The log had page after page of entries. People are so good, I thought time and time again.

We were still waiting for my mom's body to arrive from Mexico. The second week passed, and we had the second funeral. Meanwhile, family and friends began asking when we were going to have my mom's funeral. My reply was, "Not until my dad can be there or even realizes that she is gone." The last thing any of us could bear was the fact that he was going to wake up and realize that he had not only lost his wife of 35 years and his friends—but even worse would be that all of the funerals had already happened without him and his closure had passed. We just couldn't do that.

My parents were a team in everything they had ever done. They balanced each other out and always had each other's backs, no matter what. Life had not always been easy and they had many challenges, especially the financial ones in the late 1980s. Finally, they had rebuilt their nest egg. They loved being grandparents and were so excited about having a granddaughter. They traveled the globe and rode their tandem bike. My parents had never been happier. My fear when my dad died twice at the hospital was that he was going to go to be with my mom because they were a team. The other fear was what waking up and learning she was gone would do to him.

Hour after hour, sitting by my dad's bedside, I was praying for his recovery. Faith was our lifeline. Even though we had everything you could ask for in a tragedy, the only thing that truly sustained us was faith. I recalled all those years of being dragged to church every weekend and hearing my very devout dad telling us as kids that faith was a bank you deposited in every weekend because one day you might need to make a big withdrawal and you better have a full account. As we watched our always strong dad, so frail and broken, we remembered his words about faith. We were making a very large withdrawal.

The wait seemed endless. We heard my dad mumble things about seeing the Angels play and the plastic baby Jesus in Compton. In his medically induced coma, he still spoke like someone having bad dreams. He would talk in his sleep about seeing my Uncle Dave, who had been dead for years. Each day, we waited and waited. Finally, my dad woke up. We got the call from the hospital and wanted to rush over before we realized that my dad was still very weak and didn't remember the accident.

My Aunt Sheila is a psychologist, a nun, my dad's closest sibling and an unbelievable human being. She was the obvious choice to tell my dad the devastating news. He didn't remember what happened in Mexico. We had all waited for this day. So much joy that he was alive and so much grief. Celebrating my dad was awake and his brain was functioning. Yet, dreading the horror of all of this loss. Waking up to this nightmare was unfathomable.

Although my dad was out of the medically induced coma, doctors were still not sure when he was going to be released. He still had a broken back, femur, all his ribs, a punctured lung and now, officially, a broken heart. There was no way he would be at his wife's funeral anytime soon. The decision was made to move ahead without him, as hard as that was. There were still hundreds of people that needed closure. What you realize in these strange situations is that weddings and funerals are really about everyone else.

We were exhausted, numb and being supported in ways it would take a lifetime to repay. Decisions were not our strong suit. There were so many moments of clarity in the darkness, but this message of we before me was crystal clear. When I thought about what others needed, it made me feel instantly better. That was ok because "everyone else" in our remarkable and amazing community did the same by focusing on us rather than their own personal loss with the three amazing people who lost their lives.

My mom's body arrived. My dad was awake, and now it was time to give my beautiful sixty-year-old mom a proper sendoff. My mom was raised Episcopalian, and on her wedding day, as she walked down the aisle, the priest leaned into my dad and whispered, "You didn't tell me she wasn't Catholic, that will be $20 more." My dad looked at his bride and greased Msgr. Horihan's palms in dismay. He always joked that he was warned that she cost more than the rest but was worth every cent.

Not being Catholic, my mom signed papers agreeing that her children would be raised Catholic and she kept her word. We all went to mass every weekend, attended Catholic schools and my mom was involved in a number of Catholic charities. When it came to time for her funeral, it was a huge Catholic event and, of course, everyone assumed she was Catholic.

There is something peaceful, cathartic and graceful when people come together to honor a life. I followed the casket holding my two young sons' hands, walking up the aisle where our family had celebrated so many of life's events. My sisters held each other's hands, walking behind me while we all prayed that the water didn't break on my very pregnant middle sister until after the funeral. Over a thousand people were there to celebrate my mom.

The program said, "The greatest gift one can give the world is a life well lived." As we listened to people talk over and over, we were reminded that my mom knew how to live. She knew what mattered. Taking care of one another. She was present, she laughed, her smile lit up a room, she loved to have fun, to entertain and have family and friends around, she used china for hamburgers, she celebrated, was a dear friend, supported so many, mentored so many and was loved by all. Even in her death, she was teaching everyone how to live. Twenty years later, people still tell me how impacted they were by her funeral.

Rebirth

The crazy thing about funerals is that once they are over, everyone leaves, and it is quiet—very quiet. The silence was almost deafening, and it was interrupted by the phone. Who was calling at 5 am in the morning? It was my brother-in-law calling to say that my sister's water had broken, and they were heading to the hospital. The same hospital that my Dad was still recovering in. Erin and I dashed to meet our sister. We were in the room when our niece entered the world. The crying we heard now was not our own, instead, it was the cry of our niece as she entered the world. The circle and miracle of life less than 24 hours from the funeral. It all began with a loss, and now it was time for the rebirth. My dad was wheeled downstairs to see his granddaughter, and as they placed her in his arms, tears poured down all of our faces. We felt my mom's loss and her presence so profoundly in that moment. How could we experience such joy and sadness simultaneously?

We go through life so fast. Slowing down doesn't seem an option as we rush blindly towards an unknown future in hopes of avoiding the past and present. Blindly, we run faster and faster ahead until the landslide takes us down. It is the loss where we are taken down. It doesn't matter if it's a death, a divorce, an addiction, a move, or a job. It always begins with loss.

We are all afraid of change, and yet we are all faced with it because somehow the script we wrote for our lives is disrupted. The plan and vision we had shifted and the clear path we thought we were on has been blocked by a landslide. *"Time makes you bolder, even children get older."* I have realized that the gift of loss is growth. The earthquake brings rebuilding, the forest fire renews the soil and the forest, while death, grief, and loss bring rebirth. We, humanity, are ready for a rebirth. The rebirth is happening inside each of us as we gather to pick up our pieces and attempt a try at a new script, a new normal. *"Mirror in the sky, what is love? Can that child within my heart rise above?"*

What more will come from our rebirths? As we dig out from the landslide and begin to climb the mountain once again.

To be human is to love, to lose and to build again. Loss is the fertilizer of renewal. While we all try to run and avoid loss, it finds us. There is no escaping it. Our loss that November ripped a hole in our hearts, our family, our friends and our community. My dad's dear friend survived being in Mexico but did not come out unscathed. He was brain-damaged and would spend his life in a wheelchair, not being able to speak. Every couple in the accident lost a spouse. Three were dead, and one was brain damaged. The loss was not just for our families but for three other families as well. Fathers, mothers and friends are all gone in the blink of an eye. Leaving pain, grief and shock in their wake. The landslide had taken out so many.

As November 2002 came to an end and Thanksgiving was fast approaching, my sisters and I slept in our childhood home without our parents, without our spouses and me without my children. We stayed to help my middle sister and her newborn, while her husband tried to wrap up the construction at their house so they could move into their renovated home. The beautiful baby girl had come early, and they were still a few weeks away from moving back in. We were numb, in shock, exhausted by grief and taking turns in the middle of the night with our beautiful new niece.

My dad was still in the hospital, dinners still arrived from friends, and we were living in a time warp. My in-laws and husband had our sons, and I was bouncing back between my home, the hospital and my parents' home. Everyone was on pins and needles, dancing around the topic of Thanksgiving. We were all running on empty, with everyone trying to focus on caring for someone else rather than dealing with their own loss and emotions. It had been over three weeks of hell, but my dad was getting better. The best we could muster for Thanksgiving was ordering dinner via takeout. We decided we would celebrate, if that word was even possible, at my parents' house, which had become home-base.

Thanksgiving

We went to the hospital Thanksgiving morning to try and cheer up our dad. The doctor shocked us by saying that he had something for us to be grateful for this year. "Your dad is going home today, Thanksgiving

Day." The word Thanksgiving felt like a placeholder in life. Thanksgiving just hung in the air like a word we no longer understood. Thankful? The mix of emotions was so hard to process. Shock, joy, tears and celebration. We were terrified of how to help my dad with so many broken bones, a broken back, a broken leg, and most of all, a broken heart. Yet, we were giddy that he was coming home and, most of all, grateful that he was alive. It was the beginning of finding gratitude in the face of loss and adversity—learning that sadness and joy can coexist. There was much to be thankful for in spite of all the loss. It was one of the best Thanksgivings ever! Takeout turkey had never tasted so good, and our joy of being together was real. We somehow knew that my mom was smiling down on her family and new grandchild together at her table, even though the other end had never been so vacant.

The Aftermath

At 35 years old, I had lived through a handful of setbacks and challenges in my young life, but nothing prepared me for grief. My parents' financial setbacks in the 1980s and my dad's subsequent open heart surgery felt like tiny blips on life's radar after my mom's death. There is nothing that can ever get you ready for grief—nothing. It's a little like being pregnant and no one telling you about the mucus plug, and even if they told you, you wouldn't get it. Nothing can ever prepare for a loss so primal and so brutally painful.

The shower, the pillow at night and the car alone became my most dreaded places. The waves of grief would come crashing so hard, so violently and so unexpectedly. There was no controlling it. It was so bad that I had to tell my little boys and my husband that when Mommy started to cry, please just stop what you're doing, say nothing and hold her hand or hug her until it passes because Mommy misses her mom.

My sister Erin left her job and life in Orange County to move home to take care of my dad. My middle sister had finally moved into her remodeled home with her newborn daughter. I returned home to my husband and little boys. Life goes on. Yet, any smell, song or memory could take me to my knees in a second. Each of us grieved alone. Grief is the loneliest process even if we all lost the same person. Each one of my sisters and my dad grieved silently and independently of each other.

As hard as grief was, there were little glimmers of light. The sadness slowly brought a new clarity on time, the precious gift it is, how little we have and the best way to spend it. My dad was still healing and now walking slowly with a cane. He was determined to walk to my mother's grave on his own, but not in a wheelchair.

On December 9th, a month to the day of the accident, we planned a private burial for my mom. My dad, now moving slowly with a walker, was determined to give her a proper Episcopal burial. The Episcopal Bishop was called. He was a friend of the family and happy to give my dad closure. Ron had gone up to the mortuary weeks earlier, where generations of my family had been laid to rest in search of a plot near my grandparents and great-grandparents. The mortuary director laughed at my husband, saying, "That part of the cemetery has been sold out for decades or longer." Then, he paused and radioed the guy working and said into his walkie-talkie, "Hey, can you check to see where that huge oak tree fell last night?" Sure enough, it fell next to my grandparents' headstones, creating my mom's plot, right next to her in-laws. The signs from my mom had begun from the moment I heard the song "Landslide" and just continued.

Standing at the gravestone, I realized that in thirty days our lives and three other families' lives were completely flipped upside down. Twenty of our family members and my dad said a final goodbye to my mom. They lowered the casket right next to my grandparents' headstones in a graveyard full of huge and mighty oaks that rarely fell. Sturdy trees that symbolize strength, longevity, and fortitude. We grew up on a street called Oakland Avenue that was lined with majestic trees and spoke of them often as kids. The symbolism was not lost that two mighty oaks had fallen, the tree and our matriarch, both we had always believed would live on forever.

It always begins with loss. I find myself thinking about loss and growth. I think many of us feel that growth comes in tiny layers added up over time and that each day's journey gets us a little closer to inner-growth. I have a different theory.

I believe life is like an earthquake where huge jolts cause cataclysmic shifts like tectonic plates to our souls. In nature, these shifts result in mountains. Inside each of us is a similar experience. When the rocking stops, we somehow come out shifted. Our vision becomes clearer, we see what is important for the first time, we learn gratitude in everything and our growth is as monumental as a mountain. It is the growth of our soul.

I know that an earthquake has leveled our family and our friends' families. I can only pray that the shift will bring the strength, foundation, and beauty of a mountain to us all.

When the landslide takes you down
Oh, mirror in the sky
What is love?
Can the child within my heart rise above?
Can I sail through the changin' ocean tides?
Can I handle the seasons of my life?
Mmm
Well, I've been 'fraid of changin'
'Cause I've built my life around you
But time makes you bolder
Even children get older
And I'm gettin' older, too

Change for Good | 59

Well, I've been 'fraid of changin'
'Cause I've built my life around you
But time makes you bolder
Even children get older
And I'm gettin' older, too
I'm gettin' older, too

Reflection

1. Take a moment to think of a loss in your life. The death of a loved one or friend, a death, a divorce, an addiction. Journal about that experience
2. What lessons did you learn about yourself during that time?
3. How did you handle the pain? How did you grieve?
4. Begin to think about a few good things that came out of that loss.

CHAPTER FIVE

When the Landslide Takes You Down

"Grief does not change you. It reveals you."
—John Green

Adrift

After carnage there is stillness. A silence settles in after an earthquake has thundered into our lives like a massive locomotive taking out everything. Tornadoes rip across the central plains with a fury, and what remains in their path of destruction is an eerie silence. Is this what emptiness sounds like? The people, the connections and even the celebration of lives lost are now gone. Everything seems lost, colorless and still. The silence of grief is deafening and is only awakened by the sound of one's own cries.

Adrift, abandoned and lost is how I felt. My dreams had me floating on a raft in a flat and listless sea, desperately looking for an anchor, for anything to attach to. Occasionally, violent storms would occur, and the waves would take me down so deep that I could barely get to the surface to gasp for air before the next one hit—again and again. Down, down, down I went. I awoke covered in sweat every night with this dream on repeat before I began to realize that this storm was grief and it wasn't leaving anytime soon.

Each wave of grief took me down. A song, an oak tree, a smell, and I could go from being in my son's kindergarten class volunteering to an uncontrollable puddle in a flash. The waves of grief just kept coming, and some months, I didn't think I could survive or function. In between these storms was the isolation of being adrift, alone and lost at sea, desperate for anything to anchor to—desperate to find a safe harbor.

My mom was my safe harbor my entire life. She was who I ran to when I was hurt, who comforted me, who told me to be strong and brave. Even as an adult, my mom was always there and the first person I turned to for anything. We spoke every day. She was always smiling, laughing and bringing joy wherever she went. Where was the joy? Where was my mom? She was the anchor I was desperately looking for, and she was nowhere to be found in this huge ocean. Day after day, month after month, these dreams, triggers and tears continued. Eventually, I realized it was just grief.

Winner, winner!

Days before my mom left for Mexico on that fateful trip, she had purchased three raffle tickets, one for each daughter, to support my mother-in-law's favorite charity. None of us had any clue about this. Then, in May, six months after the accident, I got a phone call saying that we had won. "Won what?" I asked the stranger on the other end of the phone. We won the grand prize, a first-class cruise anywhere in the world for two weeks, all expenses paid. "*What?*" I was in shock. I couldn't fathom life without my mother, nor could I imagine going on a cruise in the depths of grieving.

Since the accident, travel was not on our minds; getting through each day with three little boys and keeping it together was about all we could do. This phone call triggered a memory. Ron and my mom had been planning a surprise Christmas gift for my dad and all of us. My mom was planning on taking the family to Paris to see Lance Armstrong win his fifth Tour de France. My dad, Ron, our boys and the world were obsessed with Lance Armstrong that year, and I didn't even know about this trip.

I called Ron at work to tell him the incredible news, and he told me about the trip he and Mom had been planning. He broke down, telling me how excited she was to do this, and said, "Your mom must be up there pulling some strings to make sure that at least I get to go." I can't explain it, but I also knew that somehow she had a hand in this. There was such a sense of her presence, and I knew she was behind this.

Thirty minutes later, the phone rang. It was my high-school girlfriend, Andrea. I hadn't spoken to her since she sang the Ave Maria at my mom's funeral. Andrea had the most beautiful voice and used to sing in a number of choirs but had stopped singing for a year or two. When my mom died, I knew one of the only things she would want at her funeral was Andrea and Ave Maria. Andrea told me so kindly when I asked her to sing at the service that she just couldn't do it; it had been too long, and her voice wasn't in shape. I asked her to simply sleep on it and let me know. Andrea called me the next morning and said my mom had come to her in a dream and told her to just do her best and that was good enough. Which is exactly what my mom would have told her. Andrea sang so beautifully, and her voice was full of love and angelic. I will never forget it as long as I live.

Now, Andrea called to ask me about a charity group she was thinking of joining and I told her about the cruise we just won and about my mom's secret trip. She told me, "Heidi, this is a sign that you are supposed to go to Paris. Your mom wants you to go to Paris." I had been to Paris before with my mom and we stayed with Andrea. Andrea had gone to graduate school in Paris, spoke fluent French and ultimately got a flat there. My mom and I had so much fun with her. Now, Andrea was saying, "You and Ron are staying at my place and going to Paris before you get on that cruise." It was all surreal.

In Search of a Sign

My mom loved to travel more than anything. She had a serious case of wanderlust. My dad traveled on planes for work every week for business, and the last thing he ever wanted to do was get on another plane, anywhere. My dad wanted to sit on a beach, and my mom wanted to see the world. Once we were older, my dad started giving my mom trips for Christmas and she would head off with girlfriends to see the world. My younger sister, Erin, inherited my mom's wanderlust. When Erin got her first job at TWA, the now-defunct airline, the family flew free. It was as if my mom had won the lottery. It was hard to keep her in one place.

We went to Europe more than once, visited so many places together and had so many amazing memories. When Ron and I started looking at cruise dates for this trip, we knew we needed to listen to Andrea and start in Paris at the Tour de France. From there, we would head to Venice and get on a cruise ship for a two-week Mediterranean cruise. Thankfully, our family rallied around the idea and everyone was signing up to help with the boys. Perhaps, there was a glimmer of light in all this darkness.

At the end of July 2003, Ron and I headed to Paris and Andrea's. I was so excited about this incredible opportunity and time away with Ron. Yet, I was so nervous with foreboding ideas of what a sign from my mom would look like. I desperately wanted one, and I asked her for them all the time to no avail. The reality was that the thought scared me, too. It was as if I was torn in this place, desperate for my mom and scared.

Grief is like putting a band-aid on a huge gaping open wound. You work so hard to try and cover it up, acting as if it isn't there. We put a little band-aid on this enormous wound and pretend that everything is fine. Then, when you hit a trigger, a memory, a sound, anything that band-aid you worked so hard on securing comes flying off, leaving your huge gaping wound exposed. The vulnerability is raw and real. The thought of having that happen—if I was to get a sign—had me in a constant state between nervous excitement and terror.

We were in Paris, and as we drove through the beautiful summer streets, all of those thoughts flew from my head. It was as if we just walked out of our lives and left all of the laundry, diapers, chaos and responsibilities behind, and we just couldn't believe it was real. Tentatively walking up the stairs to Andrea's apartment, I was nervous that there would be a trigger but as the doors opened, I was clear. Ron found an English pub around the corner that had the Tour de France coverage in English. We walked the charming street until late at night, looking for our perfect place to see the finish and complete my mom's wish.

We went for a run along the Seine the morning before the Tour got to Paris. On our run on the Champs Elysees, it began to pour rain. We ducked into the Renault dealership on the Champs Elysees to get dry. It was the coolest car dealership because it had a glass restaurant at the front window that was almost on a bridge, cantilevering over the dealership. We had found our place for the next day's end of Tour celebration and viewing.

The next morning, we made our way through the crowds to the car dealership, got a table and a perfect spot and settled in. The peloton came whipping around as we were drinking champagne, the mood was so festive and celebratory. We had an incredible time being there in person to cheer on our country and see something we had only watched on TV for so long. After the final lap, we headed down to where so many Americans had gathered, and we all began singing God Bless America. It was the most beautiful moment, and tears poured down my face because I knew my mom had somehow made this moment possible for us.

The next day, we flew to Venice and boarded our huge cruise ship. We had a beautiful room at the back of the ship by the pool. Having never been on a cruise, we were like kids exploring the huge ship along with the international crowd on it. So many of the places we were going to I had been to with my mom, and I worried at any moment that the band-aid would rip off and I would receive a sign.

The Sign

City after city on our stop, nothing. No signs from above in Paris, Florence, Venice or Rome. Finally one stop from our final destination, I had given up. I had believed so firmly that we had won this cruise because my mom had wanted to tell me something. Yet, there wasn't a sign. I was relieved and confused.

When we arrived in Ephesus, Turkey, I was no longer worried because I had never been there. I was relieved because there certainly wouldn't be a memory to trigger the waterworks I so often fought back. Because we had no idea what to expect in Ephesus, we went with a guide through the ancient city.

You might have thought that by going to church every weekend of my life, I would have recalled the Bible readings of St. John to the Ephesians. Or I would have known that when Jesus was dying on the cross, he is believed to have asked John the Baptist to get his mother to Ephesus to keep her safe. Nope, I was clueless. We listened as our guide wove the history of Christianity, Judaism and the Muslim faiths into a beautiful tapestry that, if all could hear, there would not be any religious wars. He was mesmerizing.

Then he took us up a hill to Mary's house. Yes, *the* <u>Virgin Mary's house</u>. Really? How did I not know about this? The Pope had recently made it an official site of pilgrimage. I stood in front of Mary's little brick house and smiled for a picture, not knowing what was about to happen. I walked into the darkened, tiny room with a stone floor and was struck by the most overwhelming feeling. Tears streamed down my face, I could not speak—which lasted over 2 hours—and the emotions were so overwhelming, unexpected and powerful. Love is the only word that would explain how I felt, overwhelmingly loved. Never in my life had I had a feeling or experience like this.

Was it my mom? God? Mary? I didn't and still do not know. My husband asked me if I wanted holy water, and I nodded yes. He asked if I wanted to write on the wishing wall, and I nodded yes. He asked me if this was why we won the tickets for the cruise. Tears streamed down my face like a faucet as I nodded yes. I knew for some unexplainable reason that I was supposed to be there at that moment. A girl from LA with three small sons halfway across the globe, and I was meant to be in Ephesus, Turkey. My mom had brought me here for a reason. I believe it was her way of telling me that she loved me and she was ok. I got the message loud and clear.

That moment changed my life. I now know without a doubt that there is a power in the universe greater than us all. Whether you call it God, Mary, love, light, spirit or the love of a mother... It doesn't matter, but I know and believe it is real. Since that day over twenty years ago, I began to see things more clearly, it was as if the dark glasses came off, and light began to sink into my being. That moment redirected me to make choices that align with my soul. In turn, those choices were the stepping stones towards healing, helping, service and purpose. I believe in the plan that has been set for me. My faith was reaffirmed, and a new peace came over me. "Faith is unseen but felt, faith is strength when we feel we have none, faith is hope when all seems lost." — Catherine Pulsifer

Build It, and They Will Come

Life changes in a blink. One moment, I'm with my mom, in another split second, she is gone. I'm living a nightmare adrift and drowning, and then, like someone coming up from the depths of the ocean, I break through the water and am gasping for air and light. I feel this power and love that's indescribable. I returned home, knowing I had turned a huge corner in my grief. I still felt lost, but I had a renewed sense of hope and a belief that somehow, in some way, things were about to get better. They already were.

In that first year of grief, there are so many firsts. The first month since the death, the first birthday, the first Christmas, and each first is a dreaded ordeal. Each first is a milestone and a marker that we somehow overcome, and with each passing event, we get a little stronger as we brace for the next. We were in the midst of planning for the one-year anniversary along with Ron and my dad's birthday the day before when I received an unexpected phone call from my friend Father John Sigler.

Father John went to high school with Ron. He had baptized all of our sons and had become a dear friend of mine over the years. John was a priest and acting Catholic Chaplain at Children's Hospital Los Angeles. He was calling to tell me he needed my help. Help? Did he have this backwards? People call priests for help, usually not the other way around. What could I possibly do to help Father John? John went on to explain that the hospital had hundreds of thousands of children through the hospital doors each year, and he needed help. What kind of help? John asked me if I could bring some friends down to the hospital in the next day or two. You can't say no to a priest, or at least, I couldn't, so I agreed to go.

But first, I had to get through Ron's and my dad's birthdays on November 8th, which, unlike the previous year, wasn't the happiest of occasions. That was followed the next day by the one-year anniversary of the accident. A mass in celebration of the three lives lost was planned by all of the families, and a dinner was arranged. It was surreal what one year had done to all of us. So many lives were irrevocably impacted by one bus driver's decision to make a left. We celebrated those we loved and ourselves for surviving the pain of loss. We made it, and it felt like we did cross some sort of finish line. It was a horrific year, a year of magical thinking and an incredible time of loss and growth.

Two days later, ten of us made the trip to Children's Hospital Los Angeles. A place I had never been to and only heard of because of the remarkable work they did. Father John met us in the lobby as we watched wheelchairs filled with young children being pushed by doting parents pass us by in the lobby. There was a joy about the place that seemed happy and upbeat, not morose at all. I immediately felt inspired just being there.

Father John and his boss, the Reverend Dagmar Grefe, toured us through the hospital. Telling us about the number of patients that come into the hospital and how there was no one to sit with a family when a child arrived via helicopter, to give a child a blessing before surgery or sit with parents, no one designated for end of life, to provide emergency baptisms or to support the staff when a child went home healthy after a long stay. The nurses and doctors were doing an outstanding job taking care of the patients' health—but who was there giving families that lifeline of faith and hope? Reverend Dagmar and Father John were abundantly clear that this wasn't about religion, this was about faith. This was Spiritual Care.

I was not familiar with the term Spiritual Care, but I had just lived it almost a year to the day of my visit. While I didn't know exactly how it worked, I knew that faith had been our emotional lifeline only 365 days ago. I very clearly understood the need, especially for families with children who were very ill. Father John went on to explain that he was at the hospital Monday through Friday from 9 to 5 and that there wasn't anyone there to greet a helicopter or provide emotional and spiritual support to a family at night or on the weekends. Father John was still working in his parish and had weddings, mass, funerals and baptisms in addition to trying to meet an enormous need at the hospital. He needed help.

As the ten of us stood in the hospital halls, a woman came charging at us, running and pushing a wheelchair with a little boy screaming, "Father John! Father John! I have the best news!" Father John replied, "Whoa, whoa. Take a breath. Before you tell us the news, these are my friends who are here trying to help me." The woman begins to tell us her story. She tells us that she is new to LA and has no family here, just her and her son. The young mother tells us that she was taking her son to school at the drop-off line when he was run over by another car and not expected to live. Her son was heli-vacated to CHLA and met by the medical team and Father John. She went on to say that Father John sat with her for 8 hours of surgery. He prayed with her and gave her hope and faith. Then he came every day to visit and was her emotional lifeline.

We all stood there in the halls, listening to every word of her story. When she concluded, she said, "Father John, my son is going home on Thanksgiving Day!" The words hit me like a lightning bolt— Thanksgiving Day—the same day that my dad had gone home exactly a year ago. After the cruise, I stopped believing in coincidences and knew this was more than serendipity. It was a call to action. Again, was it God? My mom? I didn't know, but I knew that it didn't matter. These women and I were starting a nonprofit to provide chaplains of all faiths at Children's Hospital Los Angeles. And that was just the beginning.

The ten of us were stay-at-home moms who all had careers before our children showed up. None of us went looking to start a nonprofit, it came looking for us. Once we committed, there was no stopping us. Our name. The Spiritual Care Guild. Our mission is to provide chaplains of all faiths 24 hours a day, 7 days a week. Our logo is a hand-drawn angel by one of our children, with stars. Our slogan: "One Spirit, one soul, one child at a time." We set the bar really low and said if we just helped one family by providing a chaplain, then that was enough for the first year. We applied for our 501c3 nonprofit tax-deductible status, and we were off to the races in November 2003.

Being an entrepreneur involves a multitude of tasks, and being chosen as the group's leader requires another list of skills. We needed a plan, a goal and a vision. Next, we had to communicate that goal to get everyone excited about what we were doing. This was pre-social media, so it was a good old-fashioned word of mouth. Our team of ten was composed of amazingly talented women who had finance degrees, had sold insurance, ran advertising and marketing campaigns and had so many talents and skills. We needed to create roles and responsibilities. Most importantly, we needed to serve the families, the patients and the staff of CHLA.

Then things got real. We asked the wonderful people at the hospital about money, stamps, envelopes... you know the basic things you need for a business. The answer was that the hospital would help us with our taxes and good luck. With no money to hire chaplains, we were going to need to get creative. We decided to have breakfast at a private club downtown, that way, we could float the bill for at least thirty days. The ten of us each pitched in twenty unique names and came up with a guest list of 200. We decided Father John and I would speak. Mary Dee, who was the head of patient care services, would also speak about the need for chaplains. One hundred women came, and one hundred women joined our group and wrote checks for their membership in the Spiritual Care Guild. We were off to the races.

Changing a one-hundred-year-old institution is like turning the Titanic. It hadn't even occurred to us that this could be difficult. Our intentions were pure, our skill sets solid, our enthusiasm was ridiculous and now, armed with 100 incredible members and volunteers, there was no stopping us. Reverend Dagmar had a tiny office, and the hospital chapel was smaller than a closet. I remember asking Dagmar, "What would a perfect department look like if you could dream any dream?" She replied, "If our Spiritual Care Department team could become accredited, then we could become a teaching resource for future chaplains or CPEs (Clinical Pastoral Educators)."

I asked what that meant in English. The translation was that because the hospital was connected with USC, if we became accredited, then every chaplain we raised money to hire could, in turn, take 5 students under them at an hourly rate while they learned to be chaplains. That way, our funds raised could pay those CPEs (student interns) hourly to cover the nights and weekends. This was brilliant! Building a department was possible. Dagmar really went to work, to create a curriculum, envision this department and become accredited. Now, we just needed to raise money. If we built it, I knew they would come.

The Signs of Angels

People often say crazy and weird things when someone dies. They are nervous and uncomfortable. It wasn't that I was getting used to it, but it happened enough times that I just braced myself for an unexpected comment or remark. One comment that really stands out was a phone call I received within days of my mom's accident from my girlfriend, Mary Grace, from Texas. She called and was very clear in her sweet Southern drawl that she needed me to listen to her, and what she was about to say was going to sound strange. She went on to share a personal story about losing someone she loved in a car accident. Mary Grace said, "Heidi, you need to look for the signs. You will know very clearly what they are, but you must look." That's when things got weird. The proverbial "they" say that when you are in your flow or on the right path, you get signs that keep showing up to say you are going the right way. So many crazy things began to happen that these signs were the only explanation.

The Spiritual Care Guild was going to have a benefit, and the theme was Field of Dreams. I cold-called a mother at our school who had an actual regulation baseball infield in her backyard to ask her if she might consider hosting our first event at her home. In hindsight, such a huge request coming from a stranger. Her name was Linda, and her husband's name was Angelo, like our logo, the Angel. When I called and told her

72 | The Transformative Power of Giving As The Ultimate Cure

what we were doing for the hospital with chaplains, there was a very long, uncomfortable pause. Linda said after what felt like forever, "We don't host events at our home, we are very private. Did you know that we lost our daughter at CHLA when she was 2?" I was instantly so sorry I had asked. I knew that band-aids of grief could be ripped off at any time, and I had pulled hers off.

Linda said, "Let me talk to Angelo, but I would love to support you and love what you are doing for families." I had tears pouring down my eyes. She then said, "What exactly did you want to do? How is this party supposed to work?" I said, "We are just getting started and trying to raise money without money, so we were hoping to serve hot dogs, use the batting cages, have a small auction and show the movie on a huge blow-up screen. We envisioned people bringing folding chairs, having kegs and maybe having local Boy Scouts throw peanuts and cracker jacks. And if we can get some real corn and turnstiles that would be amazing. Well, that is our vision." Linda replied, "Would it help if the Angels came?" Stunned, I replied, "As in the baseball team? Like real, live Angels?" Linda said, "Yes, the real Angels, the team manager is a good friend of ours." My mouth was hanging open. There wasn't one sign, there were four and all in one phone call. Sign one, they lost a child at CHLA. Sign two, the homeowner's name was Angelo, as in angel. Sign three, our logo was the angel. The last sign was that these gracious hosts knew the Angels baseball team! It was nothing short of a miraculous call to a stranger who became a fast friend. This family was angelic and the signs just confirmed it.

The day after that phone call, I was in the grocery store and ran into a friend. She said," I hear you are having a Field of Dreams benefit. Is there anything I can do to help?" I was so touched and said, "If you could just come, that would be amazing." My friend replied, "Do you want me to see if Kevin can come?" My reply was, "Kevin, who?" Her reply was, "Costner. You know, I've been working for him for years." Again, mouth open, staring at my sweet friend, I replied, "That would be amazing." She said she would check his schedule and, at minimum, have him sign things for our auction, which she absolutely did.

The signs just kept coming. Another old friend I ran into named Richard used to own a party rental business. He had sold his company but said, "I think I have a friend that can get you turnstiles and tables." And he did! A mom friend from my son's class asked me, "Do you need anything for your event?" My reply was, "Corn, I really want people to walk into a cornfield before they enter the turnstiles onto our new friend's baseball field." The mom replied, "Well, Doug works in produce, let me see if he can find corn." I received a call two days later that they would be trucking in a huge truck full of corn stalks. Sign after sign, miracle after miracle, these types of unexplained things just kept happening over and over. I knew there was a greater power behind this magic showing us the way.

The day finally came, and we had sold out our event. The weather was perfect, and all our volunteer members helped set up for two days. Placing corn in specially made corn stalk holders, so we had rows of corn walking into the Field of Dreams. There was a huge inflatable three-story movie screen. We had batting cages, hot dogs, kegs and families on their picnic blankets and folding chairs. The local newscaster in LA, Dallas Raines, was our MC and was amazing. That day in LA was the Freeway series when the Dodgers played the Angels. We really weren't sure if any baseball players were going to show up but when the bus full of Angels pulled up, I about fell over. The Dodgers sent their old-timers like Steve Garvey, Ron Cey and a few others. All the teams brought free hats and lined up to sign and give them to the kids. It was magical. When the auction and dinner were over, the movie started. We honestly thought that it would just be a nice background for people to socialize on this warm May evening. Instead, silence descended onto the baseball field as peanuts and popcorn were distributed. Every single person stayed until the movie was over and gave it a standing ovation. The night was a huge success! We raised way more than a chaplain's salary that night, and our nonprofit was off to the races.

We felt this incredible love from a new community we were building. Everyday leading up to the events, we were reminded of the kindness and generosity of people. This kindness created a bond and a strength. People think of kindness as being soft when, in reality, you become stronger with it, near it or around it. Being witness to people choosing what they want to put back into the world was magical. Feeling this pull of good, I was watching people become catalysts of change for others with each small gesture. Together, witnessing this kindness and generosity was humbling, inspiring and filled us all with such hope. People are good. Everyone who was involved felt this indescribable sense of peace, joy, connection and community. The feelings you get when you help someone. We were addicted and knew this was just the beginning.

Faith is seeing light with your heart, when all your eyes see are darkness.

Reflection

1. Think about a time when you got the chills.
2. Have you ever run into a friend you were thinking about? List some times in your life when something happened that you can't explain.
3. Think about a time when you were really stuck and didn't know which way to go in life. What did you do to move forward?
4. What would you do now?
5. Have you reprogrammed yourself to look and listen when you are being shown the path?

CHAPTER SIX

When Your Soul Speaks

"None of us will ever accomplish anything excellent or commanding except when he listens to this whisper which is heard by him alone."
—Ralph Waldo Emerson

When your soul speaks, *listen*. Sometimes, the noise around us is deafening. The sounds of children, the TV, and our phones can drown out the whisper of our soul. When we pause and search for silence, it is there. The voice we long to hear, the voice from within, guiding us towards a greater purpose. What is amazing is that we turn this voice off and tune out instead of tuning in. Our soul knows which way to go and, for me, it took the emptiness of grief, the slow signs of faith and healing to begin the process of tuning in and tuning out. It was the process of rebirth.

A huge part of me died with my mom. My inner child no longer had a mother and had to become one. It is the circle of life. The ties that bind are released, and new ties are established. Once the umbilical cord is cut, the birthing process is complete. The rebirthing process felt similar. The feeling of being adrift dissipated as a new anchor was set within. My safe harbor was no longer my mother but myself and my newly found stability. I had released my anchor and had dropped a new one deep within. I was safe again and no longer adrift. The anchor was new and still in silty sand. The strength of that anchor had yet to be tested by storms, but it was holding. The voice within guided me time and again towards deeper footings. One whisper at a time. Was it my mother's voice or my own? Whatever you want to call it, the miracles just kept happening.

Divine Timing

About a year after starting the Spiritual Care Guild, days before Thanksgiving, I received a call from Father John. He said that he had a little girl patient who was terminally ill, and her parents wanted her to have her First Communion before she died. John asked me if I could track down a white First Communion dress size 14 and hurry. I said I would see what I could do, but I was in the middle of a Thanksgiving food drive for another organization I was helping. I called a few bridal stores and they couldn't help me. I reached out to friends with daughters, but they didn't have a white dress the right size.

I made a stop to pick up food for the drive. My friend Virginia asked, "Are you ok?" I told her the story of the little girl, and she ran upstairs, returning with the most beautiful white veil. I thanked her profusely and went on my way. My next stop was my friend Meshell, who owned a jewelry store and was helping with the food drive. I shared my story and asked if her daughter might have a dress that size. She didn't, however, she ran into the store and wrapped up a tiny diamond cross on a chain for the little girl. I ran into the market to pick up food that we needed for the Thanksgiving sponsorship and mentioned the story to our local baker. She provided a beautiful cake for her First Communion. I was ready to call John to say I didn't have a dress when my girlfriend, Carol, called. She has three daughters and had made so many calls trying to help me find this First Communion dress. Carol said, "You are not going to believe this!" She had just received a care package from her family in Virginia for her three girls. When she opened the box, on top was a beautiful white dress, size 14. It was a miracle. I called John and said I was on my way to meet me in front of the hospital. He came out, and I handed him the veil, the dress, the jewelry box and the cake. John said, "How did you do this?" My reply was, "I didn't do any of this, it just happened."

John walked into the young girl's room, she had lost her hair and he presented her with the dress, the veil and jewelry box. Her parents were crying, everyone was crying, and they had a beautiful celebration. So much joy despite the illness. Another Thanksgiving miracle had occurred.

John and I spoke after Thanksgiving, and he asked if The Spiritual Care Guild could try to help families that needed emergency baptisms. I said, "What do you need?" Father John went on to explain that the hospital only had a paper stole to use, and these baptisms were oftentimes performed alongside Last Rites.

I saw my dad later that evening and told him about trying to create some sort of Baptismal kit. My dad had spent his career in the paper recycling business and said, "Let me call my friends over at the box company." I went to a meeting for a group I belonged to that had a knitting circle. I mentioned that these newborns and often toddlers had high-end paper towels for their Baptismal stole. The women said, "Give us the dimensions, and we will knit them for you." Then I spoke with my son's second-grade teacher and asked if her class could make First Communion cards for the kids at the hospital. My dad found beautiful boxes, another member of the group had candles donated, one donated disposable cameras, and our church donated holy water bottles.

The Spiritual Care Guild members got together and assembled these Baptismal kits for the hospital. Father John said, "Now when we start a baptism, we begin the ceremony by saying, another child loves your child and made this card, another person loves your child and knitted this stole." Chaplains grab the kits when they get called to families' bedsides and more than a few families have told us over the years that the ceremony and love in each item made the moment a special one for their family. Tiny steps made by each person collectively have made lasting, treasured memories for families as they celebrate in a hospital. So often, the littlest things make the biggest difference, and knowing that your life had the tiniest part of making someone else's life better is the best feeling in the world. Each act of kindness healed me, inspired me and made me want to do more.

These acts of kindness made me begin to see things more clearly. It was as if what really mattered to me before was no longer important. I began seeing the power of connection and community to truly change lives. So many times, things happened that didn't make sense, connections that I couldn't explain. There was a divine presence to it, and it just kept happening.

One of those experiences happened after that first year as President of The Spiritual Care Guild. Children's Hospital Los Angeles has thirty individual nonprofits that support different projects at the hospital. Each year, there was an annual meeting where all the presidents gathered to learn what the others were doing and report on their work. I proudly reported that we had become an accredited department and, as a result, had hired one full-time chaplain and five chaplain interns. The result was that for the first time in the hospital's 100-year history, we had chaplains 24 hours a day, seven days a week, and that was just year one!

After my brief presentation, a woman came up to me and said that she wanted to join our nonprofit. She introduced herself as Christie Houser. She was beautiful and just radiated joy and an inner beauty that lighted up a room. I asked Christie, "If you are at this meeting, aren't you already the president of a nonprofit group that supports CHLA, why would you need to join another?" She replied, "Maybe you're right, I really think I want to be a chaplain." I wasn't really sure what to say to this beautiful, young, blond mom of two, but "Wow, we sure need chaplains. Let me connect you to Dagmar, who runs the department." The next thing I knew, Christie was one of our chaplain interns and going to school part-time, studying to be a Clinical Pastoral Educator.

Christie was studying hard, working with Father John and Dagmar as well as juggling her young family. After completing all of her coursework and the required number of hours as a student, Christie was ready to make patient and patient family visits on her own. In one of her first solo visits, Christie entered the hospital room to a familiar voice. She walked over and turned off the CD player with the Disney Princess album looping. The girl's family explained that the beautiful four-year-old had terminal bone cancer, and the only two things that gave her comfort were her pink fuzzy blanket and her Disney Princess soundtrack.

Christie said to the family, "You are not going to believe this, but that's my voice on that album. I recorded this album, and I want to sing the songs to her in person." The family was stunned when Christie began to sing, and sure enough, it was her voice. The chaplain who had come to comfort their daughter was actually the voice that gave her peace. Christie sang to that little girl that day and every day until she passed, and then she sang at her service.

I no longer believed in coincidences because this was not just mere serendipity, this was so much more. The divine timing and miracles just kept happening. Each event since winning the trip to Europe, the Angels baseball team coming to our fundraiser, the First Communion dress and now Christie and Disney Princess was a sign that I was going in the right direction. Signs that I never before saw were now everywhere. My vision was crystal clear and my soul, intuition and inner voice were telling me loud and clear that the only path forward was to help others. That is the unexpected path that began to open up in new and expansive ways towards healing and purpose.

Each sign opened up new worlds that I continued to enter. I had gone through life in a relatively unscathed bubble, thinking that my insular world was the only one. My little suburban world was the only world that I really knew. Then suddenly, one day, that bubble burst. Suddenly, you are exposed, vulnerable and now pushed out into a bigger new world. In the five years of getting Spiritual Care Guild running, this new world showed me suffering, pain, joy and healing. Now my eyes are wide open.

Changes

The Spiritual Care Guild continued to grow, and so did the department. Over time, Dagmar continued to hire new chaplains that the SCG paid for, and each Chaplain took 5 new students underneath them. As predicted, the Spiritual Care Department grew out of its tiny office space. Chaplains continued supporting families and more and more were helping to support the incredible nurses and doctors at the hospital who also needed support. The chaplains began providing Tea for the Soul, a tea cart that would arrive at the same time each day at certain floors in the hospital, like the 4th floor for oncology. The cart was filled with little notes and affirmations, along with an assortment of teas and homemade cookies made by Spiritual Care Guild members. These homey touches and the calming listening presence of the chaplains gave the staff members a moment to recharge, to share about a beloved patient going home healthy and their loss. The change came slowly to a one-hundred-year-old institution, but it was a welcome one; we were all so proud of it.

Five years went by in a blink. I had been president of the Spiritual Care Guild unofficially for one and officially for two more years before handing the torch to another amazing co-founder. Change was good, and all organizations need change to continue to grow and thrive. Over time, the organization and the person identified as the founder can become synonymous. Thankfully, Spiritual Care had so many founders that it was time to hand it to the next one. My boys were getting older and my husband's career in real estate construction had him commuting. Ron liked to say, "Charity begins at home."

It was time to focus on the boys and their needs. We were commuting to the Catholic school that both my father and I had gone to in Pasadena. Our boys were missing out on last-minute time with friends because of our commute. So, we began to look for a place closer to our school. We ended up finding a fixer-upper in Ron's hometown. Once we found the house, the plan evolved from moving closer to the Catholic school to pulling the boys out of Catholic school and putting them in the local public school. The plan went over like a lead balloon with our soon-to-be 6th grader, 5th grader and 1st grade sons, all in tears and devastated. Despite the tears, we made the move. It was a good financial move and saved tuition funds. The boys would be able to ride their bikes to school, play in the park across the street and have much more freedom. Three months after our move, the real estate and financial meltdown hit. Our move had spared us from economic collapse. Once again, there was divine timing.

The Dream

Surviving the economic meltdown of 2007 and 2008, we somehow felt protected. While my husband's work had basically ceased to exist, our move had simplified our lives in many ways. It was a time of Little League, piles of bikes on our front lawn, ringing the dinner bell for dinner so the boys would come home from the park. Life was full of supporting our boys' schools, their sports, being a present mom, and there wasn't room for much more, or so I thought. There is a season for everything in our lives, and while I have always been involved, helped and been a team player, this seemed like a season to put Ron's "Charity starts at home" to practice.

Being a parent of three active boys led to long days and longer nights as the homework kept piling on. Parenting is hard work, and at the end of the day, I was an empty vessel with little to give. I hit the pillow, and I was out cold. I can sleep through anything. when I do remember a dream or on the very rare chance it wakes me up, I write it down and pay attention.

The dream was so real. I was interviewing people who started nonprofits. I had a TV show about modern-day heroes. Ron came walking into the other room asking if I was ok because I never woke up. I told him about my dream. I said, "I think I'm supposed to create a TV show about people who serve?" He groggily replied, "Oh, ok. I'm sure you can figure that out." I said, "How do I figure that out? I have never done this before." Ron replied, "Well, you had never started a nonprofit before, and you figured that out. This sounds much easier. You can do it. Call David, he can tell you how. Now, go back to bed."

David Nichols was our old neighbor who had been a lead writer on *Cheers*, *Evening Shade* and a host of successful TV shows. So, I woke up the next morning, got the boys off to school and called David. He said, "What are you trying to do?" I said, "I have an idea for a TV show, and I want to write it up and protect it before I explore it." David told me to go to The Writers Guild of America, the WGA, and register my show and concept. Within twenty-four hours of the dream, I had registered the idea. Now what? I listened, I got quiet and nothing. No signs, no voice and not even a whisper. So, when you don't know what to do, sometimes, the best thing is to just do nothing.

Oprah

It was May 2011, a month or so after the dream and registering the TV show. I was listening to my soul, and there was still silence. I knew this dream was a path but wasn't sure how to really get on it. I began researching people who had started nonprofits and how to write a television treatment. I came across the story of Michael Glasier and the Pediatric AIDS Foundation he and his wife had created. I drafted what I thought was an episode for the TV treatment and felt like a foreigner in a strange land trying to learn a new language with no one really around to teach me. Yet, something inside me was screaming that I was supposed to help the helpers and get the word out about all of the amazing humans on this earth. But how?

I was folding laundry and had Oprah's final episode on. Like half the planet, everyone was waiting to hear what she would say after twenty-five years. I had seen Oprah speak in person once before this moment. Friends had invited me in December 2004 to Maria Shriver's First Women's Conference as the First Lady of California. We had a table at the front of a room full of 10,000 women. It was surreal as Oprah walked out in bright red and was literally right in front of me. When she spoke, she channeled the voice of a slave woman from the 1850s, and it was literally as if someone else was in her body. The slave woman, through Oprah, told all of us that when women come together, they have the ability to turn the world upside down. The crowd went wild, and I think each of us felt like Oprah was speaking directly to us. It felt like we were in a room alone and not a room of 10,000. It gave me chills and having just been a year into the Spiritual Care Guild and watching amazing women come together for a cause greater than themselves, she was spot on.

So seven years later, I am waiting to hear what she will tell us now. What could she possibly say that she hadn't already told us? It was better than going to church. As I listened, Oprah said and I'm paraphrasing, "We all have the power to shine our light on something we care about. We all have the energy to create our own platform, community and legacy. What will you do with your platform and legacy?" Oprah went on to say, "This is what I was called to do. Everybody has a calling, and your real job is to find it." She credited God for everything and went on to say, "You also have to know what sparks the light in you so that you, in your own way, can illuminate the world. You have the power to change somebody's life."

It was as if I was hit by a lightning bolt. The same chills that went up my spine in Ephesus and in the halls of CHLA when the mother said, "Thanksgiving Day." It was the sign I had been looking for. Somehow, Oprah spoke to my soul and gave me the green light that I needed to move ahead. I was somehow going to help the helpers. I was going to follow her words and create a community, a platform, a place where I could elevate my heroes. This was my purpose. I was being called to be a messenger of service to amplify the voices of those who serve. It was time to get to work.

Charity Matters

I decided that May, after Oprah spoke, I was going to start one of these new blog things. When I told Ron my idea, he laughed. I said, "You didn't laugh when I suggested starting a nonprofit or writing a TV show. Why do you think a blog will be harder?" He smiled and replied, "Because a blog requires technology and that, my dear, is not your strong suit." Well, he did have a point, but once I set my mind to something, there was no going back. I decided to call it Charity Matters. I reached out to some sort of new online group of artists to create a logo. I registered the trademark, bought an online pre-fab website and asked a girlfriend to teach me how to use WordPress.

I worked all of June putting the website together. I was terrified, stretching myself in new and uncomfortable ways. I worked on pulling Charity Matters together and began thinking about who to talk to and wondered what I had to say? I knew I had a voice, silent is something I had never been, but I hadn't really been loud about what I believed in, and I felt vulnerable as the launch day approached. Hosting platforms,

Facebook pages and research on nonprofits to talk to, it was all terrifying, exhilarating and completely a new world. I decided that the launch day of Charity Matters would be my mom's birthday, July 17th. It only seemed fitting for the rebirth to be celebrated on the day she was born. Every year since my mom died, we celebrated and honored her at her favorite hamburger place in Pasadena, Pie N Burger. All my mom's friends would meet at Pie N Burger every July 17th at 6 pm to raise a cherry coke glass to my mom. The day had become joyful and celebratory, so I knew it was the perfect day to launch.

The first thing on the morning of July 17th, 2011, Charity Matters went live. We were off to the races. An hour later, I was on the road with my dear friend and fellow SCG founder, Lori, heading to the opening of the new hospital building at Children's Hospital Los Angeles. The original hospital building was built in 1901, and since that time, the hospital had undergone a number of building projects, but this was different. It was an entirely new tower called the Anderson Pavilion. The mayor was there, all of the hospital Trustees, generous donors, and of course, the press. Before the ribbon cutting, hundreds of people involved at the hospital were there.

Lori and I were sure that the mayor or some celebrity would begin the ceremony. When we saw the Cardinal of LA walking out, followed by Bishop Bruno of the Episcopal Church and then every religious leader from every faith tradition—the Armenian Pope, Native American Tribal heads, monks and on and on they processed. Then, Reverend Dagmar Grefe, the head of the Spiritual Care Department, asked each religious leader to bless the hospital, the patients, the nurses, the doctors and the staff. Lori and I looked at each other and knew that our group of friends had changed the culture of a one-hundred-year-old institution. Tears of pride streamed down our faces. The donors whose names were on the building didn't open the building. The hospital had acknowledged the faith traditions and embraced them, and this was an unbelievable moment. Another rebirth was occurring, one at CHLA and one within me.

Reflection

1. How often, if ever, do you sit with yourself in silence?
2. Think of ways you can incorporate or find a few moments to listen to your voice.
3. Reflect back to an experience where there was divine timing in your life. What happened that seemed serendipitous?
4. Do you remember your dreams? Do you write them down and keep a dream journal by your bed?
5. Have you ever had a dream that seemed so real that it was trying to tell you something?

CHAPTER SEVEN

The Obstacle is the Way

"The obstacle in the path becomes the path. Never forget, within every obstacle is an opportunity to improve our condition." —Ryan Holiday

Taking the Trash Out

The obstacle is the way. All of us are hit with enormous, unexpected obstacles in our lives that seem insurmountable. They stop us in our tracks. We do not know how to overcome, climb or even comprehend these giant roadblocks that appear in our path. These obstacles can be anything from illness, death, divorce, accidents or financial loss. Regardless of what the obstacle is, it is showing you a new path. You have to be willing to pause, reflect and realize that the obstacle is ultimately the way.

Looking in the rearview mirror, I now know that. When the boulder is ahead of you, panic and fear set in. The immediate reaction is to run away, avoid pain and protect yourself at all costs. We are human, after all, and that is how most of us react to any painful situation in our lives—we try to avoid it. That pain has a lot of energy that comes with it. When my sons were young, they would come home from school and talk about how someone was unkind or mean to them. Shortly after, I would see them being unkind to one another because people that are hurting hurt other people.

Pain should not be perpetuated. I started finding ways to talk to the boys about pain. I called that pain trash. When they came home and we talked about their day, I would ask, "Do you have any trash to take out?" They would share a story about whatever happened, and we would discuss different ways to take their "trash out." Were they going to jump on the trampoline to get it out? Scream in their pillow? Ride their bike around the block as fast as they could? When they were older, they learned to write it down and then rip it up and flush it down the toilet. Because pain can not be held onto. It must be dealt with before it is handed or given to someone else.

More than that, our conversations also became about creating boundaries with other people's pain. Just because my oldest son had a bad day, it did not mean that he could come home and dump his trash on me. He could share what was in his trash can, but I was NOT his trash can and would NOT accept his pain. I would find ways to help him take out his trash and process whatever was upsetting him. Teaching my sons early that they can not accept other people's pain was, in hindsight, a great gift. The boys began to be empathetic and see when people were hurting. It was as if they had a superpower to understand situations a little better and, as a result, the boys became resilient rather than receptacles for other people's trash. Their obstacles became their strength.

Learning to Recycle

My dad called himself a garbologist. When I was little and would say, "Dad, what do you do?" He would proudly reply, "I am a garbologist." Sometimes, he would tell me he was also a trash man, which, at age five, I thought was super cool. In reality, my dad started a paper recycling company in the late 1960s and was recycling long before it was cool. He spent his career recycling paper, buying paper, selling paper and was involved in a number of international paper businesses. My dad knew that trash should not sit in a can and that you could take old newspapers and make new ones. He knew what was in that trash can was valuable.

What I was about to discover was that he wasn't the only one who knew what to do with trash.

People always go in search of their own because like attracts like. When immigrants come to this country, they find their people. Most urban cities have a Chinatown, a little Italy and other pockets where people who share the same food, language and culture find one another. However, finding people who recycle pain was not such an obvious group. When I began to search out nonprofit founders, I didn't realize that these people were experts on recycling. I just knew that somehow they were my people.

Like any intention, when you decide to buy a red car, suddenly, you see red cars everywhere. Or when you are pregnant for the first time, suddenly, it seems as if everyone around you is pregnant. We put these filters on our brains where we attract and only see what we are focusing on. "What we focus on expands" is the saying. I began focusing on nonprofit founders, and they began to show up everywhere I went and thankfully, still do. What I didn't realize is that people became my greatest teachers. It wasn't about what happened to them but what they did with it. How they recycled the pain and created purpose from loss.

A few years ago, Ron and I were on a business trip in Canada, waiting for a cab in a hotel taxi line. A couple asked where we were going and if we wanted to share the cab. Since we were all heading to the same place, we agreed. We began talking about what we do. The husband replied that he ran a plumbing contracting business and his wife helped run their family's nonprofit that supports people with spinal cord injuries called the Be Perfect Foundation. I told them about Charity Matters, and they suggested that I interview their son, Hal. As my husband said, "Heidi, only you would share a cab with nonprofit founders." We chatted with our new friends, the Hargraves, exchanged information, and then we went on our way.

Hal Hargrave Jr. was not the first nonprofit founder I interviewed, but the one who truly drove home the message of recycling pain and taking something bad and turning it into something beautiful. A theme that became reoccurring in so many of my Charity Matters conversations. When I talked to Hal, he began to tell me his story.

Hal's Story

Twelve years ago, I was just graduating from high school and had aspirations of taking over my dad's business. I was set to go play college baseball at Cal State Long Beach and pursue a business degree. But, in a wild twist of fate, God had bigger plans for me and put me exactly where I was supposed to be. Some might say that I was physically weak, but I was spiritually and emotionally strong and capable of going out and serving others. I had a huge change of perception of what is important in life, and that is serving others.

After a roll-over car accident took my arms and my legs, I recaptured my heart and my mind and decided it was time to go serve. Although I was deemed a quadriplegic, I had never been so capable and able to light the world on fire. Like everybody in this world, you have that aha moment when you identify with things around you and mine was the realization of the lack of support from insurance companies and the inability that many had to fundraise for themselves because of paralysis. That was the need I had identified, and I went to my parents and said I think this is what I have been called to do.

Post-injury in ICU Care, there were over 200 people holding a vigil outside of my hospital room, and all I could think was, what could I possibly do to repay these people? That answer came about on day five in the ICU. A friend of mine named Katie came into my hospital room, and she broke down sobbing. At that moment, I realized that every action I take and every decision I make affects somebody around me. I realized at that moment that I could play the "woe is me" card or change my attitude.

I said, "Katie, what are you crying about?" She said, "You're not the same." I said, "But I am the same Hal. I have a heartbeat. I'm here. I can smile. I can laugh. I can communicate with you. Everything is going to be ok." And in that minute, she smiled and hugged me and that was the beginning of my realization that all of us have the ability to have a positive effect on people. My approach to emotional intelligence transcended at that point. I believe we can control two things in life. One is how we feel about ourselves and the other is how we behave.

I believe that this is meaningful and purposeful work. I've stopped asking, "why me?" and I've started asking, "Why not me?" Once I came to the realization that this happened "for me," I started looking through the lens that I "get to" do what I'm doing in my life. I started realizing that maybe this really is a blessing. The life that I'm living is far bigger than just me.

My parents said, "If you are going to do this, you will not expect a dime. You will give out of grace and expect nothing in return, and, as a family, we will support you through this endeavor. The Be Perfect Foundation was born overnight, nine months after my injury in 2007. The mission is to provide direct financial and emotional aid for individuals living with paralysis by providing resources for paying medical expenses, restoring hope, and encouraging personal independence through a non-traditional method of exercise-based therapy.

To me, the mantra of "Be Perfect" means being the best version of yourself that you can be every single day, and that starts with your philanthropic heart. Twelve years later, we have raised over seven million dollars for those living with paralysis, for things like medical supplies, wheelchairs, vehicles, handicap-accessible homes, and keeping people in exercise-based therapy programs.

To be quite frank about it, I fear not being on this earth more than anything because I know there is more that I have to give to this world. I have more in the tank. I have an opportunity to either live life for myself or for others. It is an easy decision every day to live my life for others. The most interesting thing about it is that I am always the benefactor, whether it is a smiling face or a new attitude. It makes me a better and more aware person each time this happens.

There is a level of excitement for me when I wake up every morning because I don't always know what is going to be. Sometimes, something seems negative because not everything in life is rainbows and unicorns. When we try to see the good in everything in life, we can always have a positive outcome with what surrounds us. There is a sense every day, philanthropically speaking, that if my face is attached to this foundation, then it better be run in the best, most authentic and sincere way possible. At the end of the day, there are two things that matter to me in life and that is my authenticity and sincerity. If you are going to be perfect, you have to get up and be the best version of yourself every day. God has great plans for me. I need to listen to him, I need to stop talking about all the problems in the world and I need to be a part of the solution.

We all believe that we are at the center of our own universe. We act to take care of ourselves and not others. We are hardwired to protect ourselves first. I have had to learn to get out of my own way and that it doesn't start with me but with others. I have to remind myself when I'm stressed to remove myself by one degree, and A) I can handle anything. Nothing has ever taken me down. B) Find a way to put others before yourself. C) Always lead with empathy, go to the depth to find out what is below someone's surface level because sometimes we don't know someone's whole story. Life is about others. D) Everyone can coexist if we always lead with respect. How you treat one person is how you treat every person.

On July 26th, 2007, the morning of my accident, the person that I was was driven by dollars and cents. It was all about how I was going to business school to make money for me, how I was on a baseball scholarship for me. Everything was me, me, me, me. Today, that word is never used. Today, I live for others before myself.

One of the major life lessons that I've learned from this experience is the things that we think limit us just might be the platform that we need to propel ourselves forward to actually help create change. We always think that we have it worse. However, maybe life gave us an opportunity, not a setback.

When we start looking at life through a lens that maybe something was preventing us from something even worse happening, we start to live with the appreciation that we have a second chance. Sometimes, these circumstances that put us into a deep, dark, and physically disabling place, actually are the opportunities that give us the tools that we need to create change in others' lives. You don't need to create change through physical activity. You can create change through intentionality, sincerity, words and advocacy.

Lessons from Hal

There are so many lessons to unpack in Hal's story on using pain as a purpose. Hal is a remarkable human. As you hear in his story, he first made a choice about his attitude right after his car accident. He immediately decided that he had control of how he acted. We do not have control of much in our lives, especially when faced with enormous obstacles such as Hal. One minute, he was fine, and the next minute, he was paralyzed from the waist down. His life changed in a split second. The one thing he could control was how he reacted and his attitude.

My husband has a poem on his desk by Charles Swindoll called "Attitude," and it reads:

The longer I live, the more I realize the impact of attitude on life. Attitude to me is more important than the past, than education, than money, than circumstances, than failures, than success, than what other people think or say or do.[2]

---

[2] Swindoll, Charles R. (1995). *Attitudes: Choosing the Food You Serve Your Mind.* Zondervan.

Hal is an incredibly special human, rare but not unique. He made a very clear choice about how he was going to live his life and control what he could, starting with how he reacted and his attitude. He reminds us that we each choose our attitude every day, and we all have the power to lift others by choosing to be joyful. The key word is choice.

I have thought about Hal Jr. a million times since we spoke. He had a profound impact on me with his incredible, unflinching optimism and grace. Our conversation has stayed with me and many times, when I have had a tough day, I find myself thinking of Hal and immediately, I smile. Hal's attitude is contagious, and when we hear him, we think, "I want whatever it is that he has."

The obstacle is a second chance, it is a rebirth and a redirection. The reason it is showing up in your life is to jolt you awake, to make you alive and maybe that pain is making you feel. What can you do with that trash? Where can you take it? How can you use it and recycle it to help others? That obstacle and roadblock is there to propel you forward. We can choose to be a part of a solution and not a problem. Interview after interview, I have met nonprofit founders like Hal, who took what happened to them and used it to create a solution for others. Hal's Be Perfect Foundation helps people suffering from paralysis transition to their new life. He gives them physical support, emotional support, they provide vehicles and help people make their homes wheelchair-accessible. It is about the people and the purpose in the obstacle. This is how pain is recycled.

We think "woe is me" when the obstacle arrives. The last thing we are thinking about is someone else. There is a process and it isn't immediate, it takes time. We need to give ourselves grace when life's challenges arrive unexpectedly at the door. We can choose to ignore them, but when we open the door, they are still outside, waiting to be let in. It is when we open the door to the obstacle and embrace it that we find the path forward. As Ryan Holiday said in his bestselling book, *The Obstacle is the Way*, "The obstacle in the path becomes the path. Never forget, within every obstacle is an opportunity to improve our condition." Alisa Savoretti is one of those people. She is a breast cancer survivor who took her pain and obstacles to heal herself and others in the process.

Alisa's story

Hearing you have cancer is a devastating moment. It's one thing to hear you have cancer, but it is another thing to realize you have cancer, you do not have insurance and you do not qualify for Medicaid. This is what happened to me at 38 years old. I had been working in Las Vegas as a showgirl and had recently moved to Florida to begin an online furniture business. I had borrowed funds on credit cards to launch Retrohome.com in 1999 when I found out I had cancer. The doctor said to take care of the cancer, focus on surviving and worry about the reconstruction later.

I survived but lived without my breast for almost three years. You have no idea what this does for you as a woman, for your mental well-being. During those three years, I reached out to organizations all over the country—government, nonprofit, anyone—who could help me to become whole again. I discovered that there wasn't anywhere to go. I felt deformed, depressed, frustrated, had mental anguish and enormous financial stress.

I went back to Vegas to work at The Riviera and the 1998 government law now mandated that their group policy could not decline me insurance in order to get my reconstructive surgery. I realized how my own self-esteem, confidence, and self-worth as a woman returned when I could look in the mirror and could see my whole physical being once again. It was my healing, a restoration in body, mind and spirit.

While I was in Vegas, I volunteered for a NAWBO (National Association of Women's Business Owners) event. I told the women from

NAWBO my story and these women rallied around me, and with their help, I was able to start <u>My Hope Chest</u> and had my 501c3, six weeks later on December 3rd, 2003.

Some days, it feels as if I am pushing a boulder uphill with a toothpick. After fifteen years of doing this at the grassroots level, I can tell you the work is very hard. What fuels me is knowing that thousands and thousands of women are missing their breasts and this shouldn't be happening in our country. Making women whole again is our mission. I think more women are surviving breast cancer and that's true, but what about their quality of life if they are not whole?

These women are sick and often lose their jobs because they can't work. They are now disfigured, deformed and depressed. The ripple effect of not being whole is devastating on marriages and families. This work has become my life's mission. I am not married, cancer made children no longer an option and for the past fifteen years, this work has been my life.

We pick up where the government programs leave off. That is why we exist. Our biggest referrals come from nonprofits such as the American Cancer Society, Susan G. Komen, and Care.org. We get referrals from them weekly and we can not tell our clients if or when they are going to be helped. They sit on a waitlist while we try to raise the funds to make their reconstructive surgery happen. Helping women to become whole again is what fuels me and just knowing that there is always a list of women waiting for us to find the funding.

I know that we have made a difference when we can help them with whatever they have asked for by the letters they send us. We help women every year in a small way, and I feel blessed that God picked me to do this task. Shining a light on this cause is SO important. Every time we get the word out about our work, it helps fund someone's surgery. We have been able to fill a gap where other breast cancer charities leave off. If there was another organization doing our work, we wouldn't do it, but sadly there isn't anyone else. The women we help are eternally grateful for all we have done and to me, that is the success.

We will only exist until there is a cure for breast cancer. Of course, the big dream is that there is a day when our services are no longer needed. Ten years from now, I dream that we have enough resources, funding, surgical partners and angel warriors that we can help women as quickly as they are referred to us. I dream of no longer having a waitlist and being able to have a more efficient, meaningful impact on these women's lives.

God had a different plan for my life. I have a quote on my desk that says, "When you come to the edge of a forest and there is no path—make one that others will follow." I feel like that is what happened with My Hope Chest. My life's lesson is that when you persevere, you will make a difference. I have refinanced my home three times to keep the funding going for My Hope Chest. I have taken extra jobs at the grocery store to fund this. I have learned that I have to persevere to help these women in any way I can. I cannot give up on them.

I think that changing even one life is important. Things are bigger than us, this mission is bigger than me, and I have tied my life to making a difference. I am grateful I was chosen for this journey. I am grateful to keep doing this work and I pray to the Lord that My Hope Chest gets to leave a legacy on this earth until there is no longer a need for our services. That is my utmost prayer. In the end, I know that I have done my very best.

Lessons from Alisa

Alisa was dealt a tough hand. We all get them, but what do we do when it arrives? How do we react? Alisa is an inspiration to us all because she refused to give up. She went three years without her breast. She was depressed, stuck and not in a great place. Others rallied around her to lift her up, and once she was up, there was no holding her back. She knew she needed to help other women like her. Alisa not only had physical and emotional barriers in her way, but she had financial barriers as well. She had to refinance her home three times to keep her nonprofit going. That is grit and perseverance, she refused to give up because she knew she was part of something greater than herself.

As the quote on Alisa's desk reads, "*When you come to the edge of a forest and there is no path—make one that others will follow.*" She created her own path despite the obstacles, and then she invited others to join her. Alisa knew it was okay to be discouraged, but she had set an anchor in her own life and there was no pulling it up until her mission was complete. That is persistence, grit and determination. She did not give up on herself or on those she had committed to serving, regardless of the challenges placed in front of her. When life gets tough, the tough keeps on going. Alisa persevered and so can you.

Reflection

1. Think of a time in your life *when* you have been faced with an obstacle, what was it?
2. How did you handle it?
3. How was your attitude? Could you have changed something to improve it?
4. Can you think of a time when you put others before yourself? How did it make you feel?
5. Reflect on a time when life was hard, and you wanted to quit and give up, but you kept going. What was that? Why did you keep going? Have you honored your own perseverance? Take a moment to acknowledge areas in your life where you have had grit and determination.

CHAPTER EIGHT

Gratitude, Gifts and Grace

"One can never pay in gratitude; one can only pay in kind somewhere else in life."
—Anne Morrow Lindberg

There is no joy without gratitude. The two go hand in hand, and you simply cannot have one without the other. In a moment of joy, you are full of gratitude for the gifts you have been given. Watching a child being born, experiencing nature, being with someone you love and playing with your dog—each of those treasured moments is an experience of gratitude when you make the choice to appreciate the moment.

Gratitude is more than just a simple "thank you." It's a powerful force that can transform our lives in profound ways. Gratitude is a critical part of our growth, our healing and evolution. The process of knowing that you have enough and being grateful for every precious breath, bite of food, night of safety, moment with a loved one and appreciation for the gifts we have transforms our lives in powerful and profound ways. No matter how little we have, there is always room to find something, even breathing, to be grateful for.

In the past twelve years of interviewing nonprofit founders, I have discovered some common themes in these amazing humans. These superheroes share more than a few traits that make them successful, purposeful and joyful. The number one trait is gratitude. I would say that most of the people I've interviewed have experienced some sort of loss in their lives that triggered them to act to serve others. Through their healing, they find a renewed purpose and gratitude for being alive. The other ten to twenty percent of nonprofit founders had either a close call in life or such a profound sense of gratitude that they knew that they somehow needed to pay it forward. Gratitude is a force that propels us forward, like rocket fuel, it can boost and change our lives in profound ways.

Operation Gratitude

Carolyn Blashek is a perfect example of someone who experienced such a deep and profound gratitude that she knew she needed to act on it. Her nonprofit Operation Gratitude's name says it all. Carolyn was literally the very first person I interviewed for Charity Matters, and her story is so riveting that it has stayed with me all these years. On September 11th, 2001, Carolyn was a young mother of two watching what was happening in her hometown of NYC, along with the rest of the world, that fateful morning. The only difference was that she was sure that her parents were in the Trade Center. Carolyn's parents had gone to a doctor's appointment on the morning of September 11th. For hours, she tried to reach them with no luck. After hours and hours of stress and concern had passed, she received word from her parents that they had been trapped in the subway and hadn't gotten to the Trade Center. Her gratitude was beyond immense.

As a result of her gratitude, Carolyn felt compelled, as did thousands of Americans, to join the service. But she was a mother with young children. As the talk of war increased in the following weeks, she found herself driving her minivan with car seats straight to every recruiting office in her suburban neighborhood, trying to join the military. She was deemed "too old" by all of them. After visiting the Army, Navy, Marines and Air Force, someone recommended she help the USO.

Her backup plan was the USO, which at the time was sleepy at best. One day, alone volunteering in the USO office, a soldier walked in, asking for a chaplain, but there was no one there. He asked if she would listen, and she did. The soldier had come home to bury his mother, his infant child had recently died and his wife had left him. He told Carolyn that if he didn't come home from this war, no one would care. The soldier said, *"I'm going back over there. I know I won't make it back this time, but it really doesn't matter because no one would even care."* Carolyn told him she did. That was the beginning of Operation Gratitude. It was March 2003.

The war was just beginning, and so was Carolyn. She was stunned and immediately wanted him and everyone who serves our country to know that the American people care. Carolyn was reminded of the care packages she sent to her son and daughter when they were at camp. She wanted her kids to know she was thinking of them and excited for their return home. That was the moment Operation Gratitude was born. Carolyn realized that care packages are the perfect way to show our troops that their sacrifices are appreciated here at home. She started from her living room, writing letters and creating 650 care packages for the troops. At the time, there were no other military support organizations, and her children were now 10 and 12.

Carolyn's son and daughter are now grown. Her son served four and a half years in the Marines and then went to Stanford and Yale to complete his MBA and law degrees. Carolyn said, "I had addressed thousands of care packages thinking I knew what mothers and families went through, but it wasn't until I addressed my own son's care package, that I truly understood."

Today, Operation Gratitude annually sends 150,000+ care packages filled with snacks, entertainment, hygiene and hand-made items, plus personal letters of appreciation, to Veterans, First Responders, Wounded Warriors, Caregivers and individually named U.S. Service Members deployed overseas. Their mission is to lift the spirits and meet the evolving needs of our Active Duty and Veteran communities, and provide volunteer opportunities for all Americans to express their appreciation to members of our Military.

Since its inception in 2003, Operation Gratitude volunteers have shipped more than four million care packages. The beauty, love and simplicity in simply saying thank you is pure inspiration.

Lessons from Carolyn:

Carolyn's story reminds us, in such a simple way, of the power gratitude can have on us to transform not only our own lives but the thousands of lives we transform when we serve others. She was grateful for her parents being alive, grateful to live in a free country and wanted to express her thanks by helping others. It was that simple. Today, Carolyn's gratitude has impacted millions of soldiers around the world.

I have been to Operation Gratitude's facility in the valley of Los Angeles and helped make care packages for our service members. I have also seen the ripple effect of Carolyn's gratitude on her volunteers who are equally joyful. Hundreds of people come together in the community to stuff, seal and organize the materials in these care packages. Thousands more volunteer to write letters for soldiers. Our youngest son was "bored" one summer when I suggested we head down to Operation Gratitude. We spent the afternoon writing letters and working with their incredible volunteers. When we were there, some young soldiers came in to help and to thank the team at Operation Gratitude. The soldiers shared how much the care packages meant when they were away from home, especially the handwritten notes.

My youngest son asked if he could take a picture with the soldiers and promised to keep sending notes, which he did. The nonprofit youth leadership organization I work for also got involved and sent a few thousand notes. Showing gratitude is contagious and is one of the best things we can spread among each other. Carolyn Blashek's work is a living legacy of the power of one person's gratitude to affect millions.

When we make gratitude a regular part of our daily routine, we can experience numerous benefits that touch every aspect of our well-being. One of the most significant benefits of practicing gratitude is its positive impact on mental health. When we focus on what we are thankful for, we shift our attention away from negative thoughts and feelings. This can help reduce symptoms of anxiety and depression.

Studies have shown that people who regularly practice gratitude report higher levels of happiness and lower levels of stress. This is because gratitude helps us focus on the positive aspects of our lives, which can create a more optimistic outlook. When we are grateful, we are less likely to dwell on negative experiences and more likely to appreciate the good things that come our way.

Gratitude can also improve our overall sense of well-being. When we take time to reflect on what we are thankful for, we often realize that we have more than we initially thought. This can lead to a greater sense of contentment and satisfaction with life. It's like filling up our mental and emotional tanks with positive fuel, giving us the energy and resilience to face life's challenges regardless of how difficult they may seem. Carolyn used gratitude to fuel her work to serve others. That fuel keeps refilling every time you help someone, your tank is automatically full again. Gratitude is a miracle fuel. Starting with gratitude is always a huge step to propel you forward.

The Birthday Party Project: Paige's story

The second step in gratitude is finding your gifts and talents so that you can share them with the world. We all strive to use our gifts for the greatest good and purpose. We spend a lifetime honing our crafts and talents and usually putting those skills into our careers. For many of the nonprofit founders I have interviewed, there is a moment when they realize that their skills and gifts can be used for a bigger purpose, one beyond their job. That is exactly the story of Paige Chenault, the Founder of The Birthday Party Project. Paige spent her career as a high-end party planner, organizing extravagant weddings and events to create lasting memories for her clients. I had the opportunity to meet Paige and attend a fantastic party to help support her beautiful mission of bringing joy to children living with the homeless.

The Birthday Party Project partners with homeless and transitional living facilities to host birthday parties for the kids that are staying there. Paige told me, *"I was on an airplane reading a magazine article about kid's birthday parties, and for almost a decade, I had been in the party planning business, so I was getting excited about my daughter's upcoming birthday and the party I was going to throw her. As I flipped through the magazine, I saw images of these picture-perfect parties thinking that I could totally do this for my daughter Lizzie. Then I put that magazine down and picked up a* Time Magazine *with an article about children living in Haiti and the extreme discrepancy between the party that I had envisioned for my daughter and what I saw this child in the article living in every single day. That was the moment that it hit me that I could do more with the gifts and talents I have been given. There were children that were out there who would never know the power of a celebration of people coming together. At that moment, I knew that I was the one to do something for these children. I do believe that we are called into service and absolutely do feel that I was called to this."*

Paige and I discussed some of the challenges she has faced in living out her life of gratitude as the CEO of a nonprofit. She said, *"I think, as founders, it is really important that we stay true to our core values and that we let those be our guideposts. I can see where it could be very easy if someone wanted us to do this and that moment that we begin to do things that don't align with our values is the moment when there are tension points. We have worked very hard to honor our core values, be good stewards of the dollars we have been given and serve our kids and families well. These are hard lessons to learn as a young entrepreneur."*

When we are grateful and keep giving, somehow, our cup keeps refilling. It sounds counterintuitive to what we are told, but it happens time and time again to those who serve and come from a place of gratitude. You end up with more than you started with. Paige went on to say, *"Our core team of volunteers, our party coordinators, host parties on our behalf all around the country. For me, those are the people that fuel me the most because when I am so tired and can't take one more call or email or whatever it is... I have the opportunity to look online and see what they are tackling on our behalf, and it is so powerful to see the way that they are giving their time and resources to serve our mission. We are extraordinary in that way because we have 150 party coordinators around the country who show up on our behalf. Some of these people have been doing this work for almost eight years with us.*

Our retention rate is really high and we have worked really hard to care for those people because these are the folks on our team who are doing the work. I have a team in Dallas, and we call ourselves the support team because we need to support our volunteers/party coordinators. I get really energized when my team comes up with great ideas to solve a problem, when we get it right and everything goes really well or when I get emails saying that this was the best experience I have ever had volunteering. Those are the moments for me that I am most proud of the work that we do.

We do have stories of impact and the ways in which our kids are impacted. I would say those moments are extraordinary and incredibly special. We have an immediate impact with our work, but the ripple effect takes ages to come back. Recently, I had the opportunity to run into someone who said to me, "Do you know you celebrated my 14th birthday with me when I was living at a shelter?" She is now the youngest intern ever at this company, and for me, it was incredibly special. This was my moment. It was everything for me.

It was a four-year gap before we saw her again, and she still spoke so fondly of her party with such detail. To me that speaks volumes to the level of work that we are doing, making lasting moments. This is what helps me overcome those hard days of the grass- roots building of this organization. We are leaving lasting effects on the children that we are serving, and that is what matters. These moments are the greatest gift that has been given.

We have celebrated over 10,000 children's birthdays in eight years and we have done that alongside 58,000 children. We have done that with the help of 38,000 volunteers, who we call our birthday enthusiasts. That is a lot of kids reached, a lot of birthday cakes—it is extraordinary to me.

We have done this with our agency partners or transitional living facilities or homeless shelters. The Ronald McDonald House is a prime example of a transitional living facility. Covenant House is a teen living facility where we celebrate children 17–23, and often these kids revert back to their childhood because they have never celebrated a birthday before. We partner with domestic violence agencies, sex trafficking rehabilitation programs and homeless and emergency shelters, which are typically 24-hour facilities.

I think I am more sure of who I am as a wife, a mother and a leader. I have always been empathetic, compassionate and a giver, and I have always given most of myself for others. I now realize that I don't have to do it all or be the hero of the story. It doesn't have to be about me, and thank goodness for that because there are plenty of others who can share in the joy of this. It is like taking off the cape and the in-charge mentality and telling people there is plenty to go around.

I think the biggest lesson for me is that we gain people's trust when we operate from a place of authenticity and vulnerability. If I were to continue along this journey with all the answers or needed to be the person with the first and last word, we would have crumbled by now. I think, for me, it was incredibly important as we brought people into the fold that I was incredibly honest from the beginning, that there was a lot that I didn't know, but that I knew we needed to do.

By sharing just who I was and what my strengths and weaknesses were with the people around us, we created a movement. People realized that I didn't have all the answers, but maybe they had a piece of the puzzle. By allowing them to do what they do best and getting out of the way, we were able to build this incredible community of magic makers that I trust, and that trust us.

That has been the biggest takeaway from this experience. When we get out of our own way and rely on the expertise of others, that is where the community is built, that trust exists in those moments, and you are able to do more. I believe strongly in the power of people, but allowing others to find out what they are capable of is even more rewarding."

Lessons from Paige:

As Paige shared, gratitude can make us more empathetic and compassionate. When we are grateful for what we have, we are more likely to recognize the struggles and needs of others. Recognizing people's strengths and weaknesses and being grateful for the gifts they bring to the team leads to greater acts of kindness and support. That, in turn, further strengthens our relationships and creates a more positive social environment.

Gratitude plays a crucial role in building and maintaining healthy relationships. When we express gratitude to others, it helps to strengthen our connections and foster a sense of mutual appreciation. This can be especially important in close relationships, such as those with family members, friends, work colleagues and volunteers.

Expressing gratitude can help resolve conflicts and improve communication. When we take the time to acknowledge and appreciate the efforts of others, it creates a positive atmosphere that makes it easier to address issues and find solutions. Gratitude can also encourage more open and honest communication, as people feel valued and understood.

Using our gifts for the greatest good

We all come to this planet with gifts, skills and strengths. It takes many of us a long time to identify what we are good at. More importantly, how do we give away the gift we possess? A couple of years ago, I had the good fortune to interview an amazing man named Don Schoendorfer, an MIT Biomedical engineer by career. Don had spent a life tinkering, fixing and building things alongside his father and brothers. He is the Founder of the Free WheelChair Mission, where he strives to help the 75 million people living around the globe without a wheelchair.

He told me, "*I always knew I was going to do something to help people. About twenty years ago, we went on a vacation to Morocco. The first day, we were in a very old part of the city, probably built during the Crusades. There were dirt roads, buildings close to each other, just wide enough for a wagon and donkey to get by. Between the legs of people commuting back and forth on foot, we saw a woman drag herself across the dirt road. She was using her fingernails for traction. And she's looking at her hands. She's not looking at anything else, but her hands, and she's very careful about how she places them. Her feet were just dragging behind her. They were just connected to her and not functioning in any way. She was bleeding and very filthy, and her clothes were torn.*

It was our first trip to a developing country, and we were shocked. Shocked at her appearance, but also shocked at the fact that people were just basically just stepping over her like she was some kind of garbage and not helping her. We went home and got on with our lives. That's what I did

Change for Good | 109

for 20 more years. Every now and then, something would remind me, or in the middle of the night, I would wake up, and I'd be thinking about that woman and the struggle she had just to keep alive."

In 2001, Don said he got a call from God in the middle of the night. Don told me that God *said, "I need to talk to you." "What about?" He said, "Why are you wasting your time?" And I said, "What do you mean?" God said, "Why don't you use the gifts I gave you to do something?" I don't want anybody to misinterpret, I do not have that kind of relationship with communicating with God. But if I summed up what I was going through, this was really what I came up with, "Hey, I'm an engineer, I'm an inventor, I can do this stuff."*

I thought, where do I focus my energy? All of a sudden, there's this woman crawling across the dirt road. What's the need, what does she need? I go to Toys R Us and I get some bicycles. Then, I go to Home Depot and I get some white resin lawn chairs. Then I spend five or six months trying to figure out how to effectively connect them together. And, it's a white resin lawn chair with mountain bike tires. It doesn't look like a wheelchair. But I think that woman probably would have loved to have something like this.

I asked Don when he knew he had made a difference. He replied, "*When I saw this family change. Can you imagine if you were carrying your 11-year-old son with Cerebral palsy? Can you imagine that this boy's parents had carried him every day of his life? His parents can't work, and therefore, they can't make enough money to live on.*

When they got their son a wheelchair, it changed their lives. The parents could work and take their son with them. They could move him to the shade of the rice paddies where they worked. Now, they can both work, and they can make enough money to advance a little bit in their economy. Even better, they now have more freedom.

Of course, they didn't know what was going to happen after we put their son in the chair. They probably thought we're going to take some pictures and then take it away from him. Instead, we drove away at the end and left that chair to them. We didn't come back and take the chair.

These people are already happy. When you give them a wheelchair, it's so profound. You can just see how hard it is for men to express their gratitude, some are just choked up, and they can't get the words out. They're just crying and smiling at the same time. The whole family doesn't have to carry anyone anymore. He can go by himself. I asked Don what he had learned from giving away over one million free wheelchairs. His answer said it all, *"There are so many other things we can do. Think about what you're good at. Maybe you get the call from God. Or maybe you don't. Ask yourself, what am I really good at? Is that what I'm doing to help people? Am I using those tools to help people?"*

Lessons from Don:

Don's story not only highlights his gratitude but also the contagious nature of gratitude to the families he has served. He reminds us to not only serve others but to use our gifts to their greatest purpose. When we do that, the benefits we receive from serving and gratitude extend beyond mental and emotional well-being to include physical health. Research has shown that people who practice gratitude regularly tend to have better physical health outcomes. They report fewer aches and pains, better sleep, and a stronger immune system.

One reason for this is that gratitude can help reduce stress, which is a major contributor to many health problems. When we are stressed, our bodies produce higher levels of cortisol, a hormone that can negatively impact our health. By focusing on what we are grateful for, we can lower our stress levels and promote a healthier physiological state.

Gratitude can also encourage healthier behaviors. When we feel good about our lives, we are more likely to take care of ourselves. This can include eating a balanced diet, exercising regularly, and getting enough sleep. These healthy habits can, in turn, further improve our physical health and overall well-being.

As Carolyn, Paige and Don told us, giving back to others can help you cultivate a sense of gratitude for what you have. Volunteering your time or donating to a cause you care about can provide a sense of purpose and fulfillment. It can also remind you of the positive impact you can have on others, which can increase your own sense of gratitude.

Gratitude is a simple yet powerful practice that can bring numerous benefits to our lives. From improving mental health, strengthening relationships and building resilience, the positive effects of gratitude are far-reaching. By incorporating gratitude into our daily routines, we can create a more positive and fulfilling life for ourselves and those around us.

Remember, gratitude is a journey, not a destination. It's about making a conscious effort to focus on the good things in our lives and appreciating the people and experiences that bring us joy. So, take a moment today to reflect on what you are grateful for and let that gratitude guide you towards a happier, healthier, and more fulfilling life.

Gratitude Homework

Practical Tips for Cultivating Gratitude

Now that we've explored the many benefits of gratitude, you might be wondering how to incorporate this powerful practice into your daily life. Here are some practical tips to help you get started:

Keep a Gratitude Journal

One of the most effective ways to cultivate gratitude is to keep a gratitude journal. Each day, take a few minutes to write down three things you are thankful for. These can be big or small, from a kind gesture from a friend to a beautiful sunset. Over time, you'll find that focusing on these positive experiences can help shift your mindset and make you more aware of the good things in your life.

Express Gratitude to Others

Take time to express your gratitude to the people in your life. This can be as simple as saying "thank you" or writing a heartfelt note of appreciation. Letting others know that you are grateful for their kindness and support can strengthen your relationships and create a positive ripple effect.

Practice Mindfulness

Mindfulness involves paying attention to the present moment without judgment. When you practice mindfulness, you can become more aware of the things you are grateful for. Take a few moments each day to pause and reflect on the positive aspects of your life. This can help you cultivate a greater sense of gratitude and appreciation.

Create Gratitude Rituals

Incorporate gratitude into your daily routine by creating gratitude rituals. For example, you might start each day by thinking of one thing you are grateful for, or end each day by reflecting on three positive experiences from the day. These rituals can help make gratitude a regular part of your life.

Volunteer and Give Back

Giving back to others can help you cultivate a sense of gratitude for what you have. Volunteering your time or donating to a cause you care about can provide a sense of purpose and fulfillment. It can also remind you of the positive impact you can have on others, which can increase your own sense of gratitude.

Focus on the Positive

Make a conscious effort to focus on the positive aspects of your life. When negative thoughts or challenges arise, try to reframe them in a more positive light. This doesn't mean ignoring difficulties, but rather finding a balance by also acknowledging the good things that are present.

Practice Self-Compassion

Be kind to yourself and practice self-compassion. Recognize that it's okay to have tough days and that you are doing your best. By being gentle with yourself, you can cultivate a greater sense of gratitude for your own efforts and achievements.

Reflection

1. Do you have *a* gratitude practice?
2. What do you think are your gifts and talents?
3. How do you use those gifts?
4. Has your cup ever felt full enough that you have enough extra to give?
5. What is one of the gratitude tips from above that you could incorporate into your daily routine?

CHAPTER NINE

We Rise by Lifting Others

*"To know even one life has breathed easier because
you have lived, this is to have succeeded."*
—Ralph Waldo Emerson

Do you remember that book called *All I Really Need to Know I learned in Kindergarten* by Robert Fulghum? It is always fascinating to discover people's earliest acts of kindness. Where did you learn kindness? Who modeled or showed you the way? Where did you learn the importance of helping others? Or is it something innate in each of us? I found myself trying to answer these questions: What were my earliest memories of charity? Where did the joy of helping come from? Actually, it is one of my most vivid early memories.

The year is 1971, I'm five years old and in Mrs. Thompson's kindergarten class. Mrs. Thompson, who might have been 100 at the time, was the sweetest, kindest woman. She asked our class to bring in pennies for the poor. I know poor is no longer politically correct, but it was the seventies. I vividly remember going home and emptying my own piggy bank and cramming a handful of pennies into my chubby hands. Mrs. Thompson was very clear that it had to be our money and not our parents. Something about using my own pennies made me so happy and proud.

The next morning, Mrs. Thompson asked the class of about twenty students, who had brought in pennies. I raised my hand along with five other students, and she called us all up to the front of the class and gave us a lollipop for every penny we brought in. It was amazing. I felt so excited to be getting rewarded but didn't understand why we received lollipops. Mrs. Thompson didn't say anything else but thanked us for caring for others. I remember feeling very proud and excited about the bonus of candy.

The next day, the remaining students brought in way more pennies than the six of us had the day before. A boy in my class asked Mrs. Thompson, "Excuse me, please, Mrs. Thompson, but when are we getting our lollipops for all of our pennies?" Mrs. Thompson very calmly explained, *"The first group of students brought in their pennies because they wanted to help poor children, and they didn't expect anything in return. Those students didn't know about the candy and just gave it to give. All of you brought in pennies to get something for yourselves and that isn't real charity. Charity is when you help someone and expect nothing in return. I want all of you to learn that when you give for no reason, that is when you are rewarded."*

I remember a few of the boys saying that it wasn't fair. To be honest, I'm not sure that I really understood exactly what Mrs. Thompson meant. What I did know is that I felt really proud to give my pennies and really excited to get a bunch of candy I didn't expect. Somehow, I knew this was a feeling I wanted again. Mrs. Thompson empowered me in a way I had never felt before. It is amazing that over fifty years later, I can remember that moment like it was yesterday. We are all made up of so many moments and life experiences that shape us and set us down certain paths. We never know when a seed that was planted long ago will sprout and grow.

More than empowering me and teaching empathy and kindness, Mrs. Thompson shifted every student's eyes to others. It wasn't about us but rather about what we could do as a class to move the needle, even in a small way, to help other children. It was the first step in my life to go from the "me" mentality to the "we" mentality.

Shifting from Me to We

Shifting from a "me" mindset to a "we" mindset can transform the way we experience life and interact with those around us. When we focus solely on ourselves, we often become absorbed in our own needs, desires, and problems. This can lead to feelings of isolation and stress, as we may feel like we are constantly striving to meet our own expectations without much support. However, when we begin to consider the needs and perspectives of others, we open ourselves up to deeper connections and a sense of community that can be incredibly fulfilling.

Thinking about others allows us to practice empathy and compassion. By putting ourselves in someone else's shoes, we can better understand their experiences and struggles. This not only helps us to respond more kindly and effectively to their needs but also helps us to develop a greater sense of gratitude for our own lives. Empathy creates a bridge between people, fostering trust and mutual respect, which can lead to stronger, more supportive relationships.

Moreover, when we adopt a "we" mindset, we often find that our own problems feel less overwhelming. Helping others and contributing to the well-being of our community can provide a sense of purpose and fulfillment that is difficult to achieve when we are focused solely on ourselves. Acts of kindness and generosity have been shown to boost our mood and overall well-being, creating a positive feedback loop that benefits both the giver and the receiver.

A perfect example of this is Dan Zauderer, the founder of Grass Roots Grocery. Dan was a school teacher in the Bronx who realized that his class had children living with food insecurity. What he did next shifted not only his own mindset but that of his entire community. It is a lesson we can all learn about going from "me" to "we."

Dan's Story

Our mission statement is to advance food justice by cultivating a community of neighbors helping neighbors. What that means in action, is neighbors coming together, in grassroots service, making sure that their fellow neighbors have enough food to eat.

There are two different programs that we do, but it's really just founded upon the notion that we all need to come together to take a bite out of food insecurity. This is not something that big food pantries can do alone. It's not something that we can just leave up to the policymakers. The problem is so big that the only way to really shift it is for everybody to be involved.

Whether it's by people roping in their corporate workplace, reaching out to their local girl scout troops or taking a couple of hours out of their week to help make sure that their neighbors are nourished and fed. That's what this is about. It's kind of a narrative shift focusing on bottom-up direct action from the people. It's basically about operationalizing this notion of neighbors helping neighbors and applying it specifically to the realm of food justice.

I started working at a school called the American Dream School in the South Bronx. The student population is the children of mostly undocumented Central American and Mexican immigrants. One day, I am walking home and I see one of my students on the sidewalk. Next to my student, I see that there's this elderly woman who's digging through trash can dumpster-diving.

So, I reached out to my student the next day and I asked him to share about what I saw. He told me that the woman was his grandmother, and this was a normal activity. When COVID hit, I thought how can I rally my family and friends around something that would be helpful to my student community? I decided that we should just raise a bunch of money because I knew it wasn't just this one student, there were other families who had to deal with food insecurity. We found out that one out of every four families was cutting down on meals a few times every week in my school community.

Then, I learned about community refrigerators. The idea is literally a fridge on the sidewalk put down by an organizer. You place a refrigerator in a local store and you get people to donate food. Then, we rallied together staff, my own family and friends and said, "Alright, let's start a community fridge in Mott Haven." That's the way that this was started, as a teacher's passion project that, ultimately, was renamed GrassRoots Grocery.

We've recruited over 3000 volunteers to help out with this work, and they light me up. Whether it's little kids, or high schoolers engaging in some kind of direct action to support their neighbors with food justice.

Every Saturday, we have what I call a "produce party." We come together with over 100 volunteers in a parking lot in the South Bronx to unload a truck filled with surplus produce that we've picked up from the Hunts Point produce market, which is the biggest produce market in the country. We work together as volunteers to unload that truck, and to sort through all the food, and we load it up into the vehicles of our volunteer drivers. The drivers bring it to our network of community liaisons.

All of our volunteers got an email saying that they moved about 10,000 pounds of excess produce to 34 different communities throughout Harlem and the Bronx, and reached over 1,000 families through community leader liaisons. Those liaisons gave out that food to their neighbors in need in the way that they thought best. That happens every weekend.

This crew of community leaders—I call them grassroots grocers—all have stories of their own. They're all doing this work for free because they're leaders in their community. They want to give food to their people in need, so they're volunteers.

The real dream is to end food insecurity. But that's not going to be in my lifetime, although, it would be amazing. My dream is that this mindset of neighbors helping neighbors to promote food justice becomes ingrained into the habits of people's lives. And it's already happening. We have families that are making sandwiches or that are taking leftover meals and putting them into Tupperware containers and filling the community fridges. People take time out of their Saturday, once a month, to join us in a produce party.

What if it just became commonplace, right? It's this idea that we all need to come together. We can't just rely on these big food rescue trucks, big nonprofits and the policymakers. It's up to all of us, even if it's just a couple hours a month. That's really my dream, is for that mentality to just wash over the world.

The life lesson that I learned and that is just so important is to have meaning in the work that I do. It's really important for me to do something that feels meaningful. I've been sober for 12 years, and you know, starting a nonprofit is even harder than getting sober.

I'm just so lucky that I created this amazing community of neighbors helping neighbors. The fact that I can do this work and light people up and get people's kids involved and spread this message. It is just what fills my cup. Centering on meaning and finding a way to remember all of the blessings of the work that you're doing is what it's all about.

Lessons from Dan

In a broader sense, shifting to a "we" mindset can lead to more harmonious and resilient communities. When people look out for one another and work together towards common goals, the collective strength and resources of the group can overcome challenges that might be insurmountable for individuals. This sense of solidarity can create a more supportive and nurturing environment for everyone, where each person's well-being is interconnected with that of the whole community. That is the place where positive change happens for everyone within the group, for the entire group as well as the recipients.

Nonprofit founders have many roles, but one of the most important is building a community. Bringing a group of people together who are inspired by you, your idea and your passion. As humans, we all crave connection and community, it makes us feel as if we belong. When we create a community and bring people together, whether it's for a cause, to support someone who is struggling or to bring dinner for a family with a new baby, that community makes us feel a part of something bigger than we are. The community creates belonging, acceptance and purpose. At their core, nonprofit founders teach us about building community, the importance of nurturing community and show us how to thrive in the community.

Dan's story is a beautiful example of what happens when one person sees a problem and decides to take action. It is an even better example of what happens when one person lights a spark that becomes a fire for good. Dan and so many nonprofit founders like him have stepped up and taken action, and they have called on their friends, families and neighbors to join them and do the same. They invite us to join their mission and their community and to go from the "me" mindset to the "we" mindset.

Another amazing person who has inspired me is the incredible Maggie Kane. A few weeks after she and I had our conversation, she ended up on The Kelly Clarkson Show, inspiring and building an even larger community with her joy and welcoming message of "come to the table." Maggie's life is all about creating community and bringing the "we" to her work.

Maggie's Story/ A Place at the Table

A Place at the Table is in Raleigh, where I grew up. So, I am biased as to how great Raleigh is. We are a Pay What You Can restaurant. So, let that sink in for a minute. There's not many of us around the country. What that means is we look and feel like any other restaurant that you might go to every single day with your friends and your family or by yourself.

But what makes us different is that you pay what you can, and all of our prices are suggested. So you can choose to pay the suggested price or you can choose to pay more and pay it forward for someone else who can't afford their meal. You can pay less because we know some weeks are harder than others, and all you can afford is less. You can also pay by volunteering with us. When you walk in, you feel like you're in that regular restaurant I was talking about. You would not know that anything's different until you get up to the register.

A Place at the Table smells delicious with bacon, coffee and cinnamon rolls. It's warm and beautiful and has great music. You feel like you're in this regular Cafe, but then you get up to the register. That is when you get to make that choice of how you pay. Our mission is community and good food for all regardless of means. The main reason we do this is to build community. We use that suggested pricing to bring all people together no matter who you are.

I'm so fortunate, I have the best job in the world. I've got the best team in the world. This is a whole community-wide effort with a twenty-person staff and thousands of volunteers that make this happen. I grew up in Raleigh and kind of always thought I would leave. I ended up going to North Carolina State University, which is in Raleigh, and it was awesome. While I was in school, I was part of a club where I heard this speaker come in who ran a day shelter.

A day shelter is a place where folks experiencing homelessness, who sleep outside, can come during the day. I heard the speaker talking about it, and I was immediately intrigued. I went to visit, and I ended up staying there every single day, working the front desk, chatting with people, and getting to know people who slept outside.

When I graduated college, I ran the day shelter and I got to know so many more folks on the street. I truly mean they're my friends. I always thought, what do you do with your friends? You eat with them or you get coffee. Food is that tool to bring people together. So, I worked with folks on the street, and we would eat at the soup kitchen. Raleigh has an amazing soup kitchen that feeds 300 people in an hour. It was at that moment when I'd be eating with them that I thought, wow, this is so different from my life experience. I can go and eat wherever I want.

I just thought we should go out for other meals and celebrate birthdays, anniversaries and really just spend that time together. My friend John changed my life forever when he picked a restaurant called Golden Corral. When I asked him why he picked it, he said, "There are two reasons. I have a choice. I get to choose if I want to order a steak or if I want a salad or if I want a waffle. Living in poverty on the streets, people make every choice for me, from what I eat to where I sleep. Second, I feel seen and heard here. Living on the streets, people literally step over me, they treat me as invisible, and here, I have value. People greet me at the door."

That got me thinking, how do we create a place where everyone can come together and build that community? I started researching, and I found the pay-what-you-can model. There are over 15 other Pay What You Can cafes across the country. I started chatting with some of these other cafes and said, "You know, if other places can do this, then Raleigh can, too."

The answer to everything in life is good people. Every moment I meet someone new, who reminds me of why I am doing this. People said this is a fantastic job and this is what the community needs. I feel like I'm the luckiest person, I said this before but I have the best job.

We opened in 2018, operating this tiny cafe, and we fed 50 to 70 people a day. At the time, we thought we were killing it. Then, the pandemic hit and we went from 50 people a day in this tiny cafe to doubling in size. We were very fortunate to expand our whole space and serve a free meal to 400 people a day. Wow, it was wild!

Now we're sitting at about 100 to 150. As nonprofits, you have to start realizing, are you actually doing what you're supposed to be doing? So, we paused for three weeks, we expanded our space, and we reopened getting back to our original mission of community and good food. Now that we got through the pandemic, we're starting to dream, which is really, really exciting.

So my dream is really to see Pay What You Can cafes across the country everywhere. And we feel lucky to have such support here in Raleigh and figured out how Pay What You Can restaurants can work in a busy downtown setting. So, we want to help other people open

Relationships are everything! I always tell people, lean on people around you for help, people want to help you. People are powerful, and it's better when you're in relationships with people. Life is better when you belong, and you make people feel like they belong.

People want to help people feel like part of something. So, do not be afraid to ask. I think the third thing is to celebrate everything! I learned very early on to celebrate that first $5 donation check. From then on, celebrate every little moment because it's more fun that way. And time is just short. We only have so much time here.

I definitely still feel the same way I did 10 years ago when I had no idea what I was doing and I was thinking, there are people going to figure out that I have no idea what I'm doing. But I have definitely grown and felt more confident in this work and just felt more love in this work than I've ever felt. Now I truly 100% know my purpose in life, and I will continue to do that until the day I die.

Lessons from Maggie

Maggie's work in bringing people together from all walks of life for a place at her table is the definition of community. Everyone is welcome, and everyone feels seen and the same. As Maggie said, "People want to help, and people want to feel a part of something." She is right. We do. We want to belong, to be together and to feel that we are working together for something good. There is no greater feeling than working together to accomplish something that helps people. It is what joy feels like.

Nonprofit founders are joyful, happy people. They inspire community and connection. They are grateful, and they live full rich lives, full of purpose and relationships. When I think of the movie *Harry Met Sally* and the infamous dinner scene with Meg Ryan and Billy Crystal, I think of nonprofit founders. You know the scene: Meg Ryan is pretending to have an exaggerated orgasm at a restaurant when the woman next to her tells the waitress, "I'll have what she's having." People who help other people exude joy, a light and a purpose that makes people say, "I want what they are having." Many times, it is that energy that invites people into a community. From there, a slow process of shifting from the "me" mindset to the "we" mindset journey begins.

It isn't an overnight process, it takes time. Mine started in kindergarten and is still developing. It took one person, Mrs. Thompson, to ask our class to help other children. To simply think about someone else. We have so much noise coming at us sometimes that it is hard to think clearly about what we are having for dinner, let alone about helping someone else. It starts with a mindset and an awareness. The goal isn't to become Mother Teresa, but when you help someone, you will find gratitude, joy, connection, and community. You will exude that light.

Reflection

1. Think about your earliest memories of doing something for someone.
2. Do you remember how it made you feel?
3. We all have moments of me, can you reflect on a moment of "we"?
4. How did you feel when working in a community towards a goal?
5. What are some activities or causes that you participate in that community? (Church, pickleball, volunteering)
6. What are some small steps you could take to get involved?

CHAPTER TEN

Learning to Lead

"There are two ways of spreading light: to be the candle or the mirror that reflects it."
—Edith Wharton

Are we born leaders? Or do we learn to lead? It is the age-old question of nature versus nurture. Many of us are born with some gifts or skills that fall under the leader label. You may enjoy public speaking or have great organizational skills. Maybe you are someone who always has a plan. Perhaps you are dynamic and charismatic? So often, as young children, we see someone with these skills and label them the leader. Over time the child believes they are a leader, and eventually, they become a leader.

But what about the rest of us who didn't get that label or those skill sets? Are we all really followers doomed to be lost for the rest of our lives? No, is the short answer. The reality is that leadership is a skill set just like any other and the more we practice the skill set, the better leaders we become. It is a muscle that has to be worked out and built up over time with much repetition and heavy lifting. Leadership is a common thread in all of the hundreds of light workers, change makers, and modern-day heroes I have met over the years. All of them are living purpose-driven lives and all of them are leaders. None of them set out to become one.

Let's face it, most of us don't want to be in charge because, honestly, it seems like a lot of work. Yet, when we are left without leadership, we are lost because leaders show us the way. How many times have you lost a boss at work, and panic sets in about who is in charge now? What will this new boss/leader be like? The same things happen with presidential elections, the PTA and your neighborhood association. Many of us panic about who will be in charge. Oftentimes, we don't realize the importance of leadership until we have a bad one or no leader at all.

In the scheme of what is important in our daily lives, leadership is something we simply don't think about, often until it is too late. Many of us, myself included, fell into the leadership role by accident. We became the leaders of our siblings because of birth order. I am the oldest of three girls, and I was put into a leadership position and helper role from the moment my middle sister arrived. I think my sisters would describe me as the bitchy, bossy older sister more than the leader. There is no denying that having that role thrust upon you at a young age does help develop some leadership skills.

Just because you managed your younger siblings doesn't necessarily make you a leader. There are a million books and opinions on the topic of leadership. Regardless of where you are in your leadership journey, there is always room to grow and learn. Often time leadership comes looking for you before you go looking for it. How many times have you missed a meeting only to find out that you were selected to take over a role you really didn't sign up for? We begrudgingly do the work, grumble a bit, and complain about how much work it is to organize everything. When the work is done, we feel great. We have stretched ourselves, taken on more responsibility and grown as a leader from the extra lifting we did. Living our best life means becoming the best versions of ourselves, and like it or not, leadership skills are skills we need to thrive and to be happy.

TACSC

When leadership came knocking at my door, I was not looking for it either. It was 2013, my sons were now in middle school and high school and becoming more independent each day. I had been giving my time to causes I cared about for over a decade, being home with my boys. It was one of the best investments of my life, with zero regrets. However, college times three was looming, and life, as we know, always seemed to get more expensive instead of less. I began to ask myself the question, *"What if I actually got paid for all this work I do?"*

At the time, I was serving on a number of school boards, and chairing one. I loved using the skill sets I had used in my pre-child life while being part of a team. Slowly, I realized from all the nonprofit work, volunteer work and my entrepreneurial work at both Spiritual Care Guild and Charity Matters that I had skills worth money. We all have an inner critic, but this time that inner voice was quiet, and I began to talk about going back to work. I updated my resume and began the process of getting active on LinkedIn. Little by little, Executive Director roles began coming my way. In any job, you want the right fit. When you are working to solve the world's problems, you really want to work for a cause you believe in.

In November 2013, I was serving on my alma mater's school board with some great people, and one of them was a terrific guy named Kevin. He is wicked smart, easygoing and always has insightful things to say. The other board I was on was an all-boys school in South Central Los Angeles. It was a Jesuit Christo Rey school, which meant that the boys went to school four days a week and worked in a white-collar office one day a week to pay their tuition. One hundred percent of these young men grow up in poverty, and all go on to a four-year college.

On that board was my friend Jim. Another brilliant guy who always had the answers to things and was a natural-born leader. I had no clue that Kevin and Jim were old friends. More than that, they were on another board for a nonprofit Catholic Youth Organization called TACSC. It turned out that TACSC's founder, a Catholic sister, had retired, and they were in search of a new Executive Director. Jim and Kevin were discussing possible candidates and both suggested yours truly without knowing the other one knew me. Serendipitous, I suppose, but since I no longer believe in coincidence, maybe fate is more likely.

Before I knew it, my two friends were pitching me to take over a then-30-year-old nonprofit that was not in great shape. The best way to describe TACSC at the time was a heart without a skeleton. Tens of thousands of incredible students had gone through this youth leadership program and loved the organization dearly. It had changed their lives, made them leaders and given them these incredible lifelong friendships and some of the best memories of their childhood. As a result, the alumni did not want one tiny thing changed because, in their 6th-grade minds, it was idyllic...most especially, a new Executive Director.

I wasn't so sure about this. Leadership? Raising money and creating an organization that helped sick and dying children, sure, but leadership? Catholic leadership on top of it. It definitely wasn't sexy, that was for sure. From what I could tell, the organization's programs were terrific, but operationally, it was a trainwreck. There was no skeleton or working systems. To give you an example, the database of the tens of thousands of alumni were shoe boxes piled high and filled with beautifully written 3x5 recipe cards with each student's information. Since I love a good challenge, and Jim and Kevin were very persuasive friends, I took the job. I told myself that I would turn this place around in five years and walk away. Little did I know that these young leaders had a lot to teach me about leadership.

Pillars of Leadership

The organization was created in 1982 to address the question of who will our leaders be? Catholic schools at the time were losing the priests and nuns who were running their schools. The idea was if we supported this newfangled idea of the Student Council, then there would be six leaders in every school. So TACSC's name comes from its original name, The Association of Catholic Student Councils. The mission is to develop moral leaders who positively impact our world. If truth be told, the real reason I took the job was not the money or the challenge but the idea of teaching or being a part of teaching thousands of students each year to be kind, to serve and to give...that felt impactful. So I became the TACSC master.

To be honest, I didn't really know that leadership had steps and pieces when I became the leader of the leaders. Who knew there was a process to leadership? Here I was worried about the lack of processes and systems within the organization and didn't understand the basic system of leadership. I know the irony is rich. There was much to learn, but one of the first tasks, pun intended, was understanding what we taught and why it matters. How I had lived my entire life not really knowing this leads me to assume that unless you have read a ton of books, studying leadership, you probably don't either. Whether we choose to lead in little ways or in big ways, we all need to be the leaders of our own lives.

We can't lead our lives if we don't know what we want. It all has to start with that vision, dream or goal that you have always wanted to achieve, to do or to become. If you remember back to Chapter Six, this entire journey started with a loss and then a dream. Never have I felt so lost, and then this dream appeared saying that I would create a television show about people who change the world, people who serve and help one another. It is those dreams, visions, and plans that guide our lives and move us forward. At TACSC, we call it being a Real World Strategic Planner, but at the end of the day, it is having a goal and making a plan, even if it's a tiny plan to put into action.

When you think about wanting something, let's just say it's a new job. You need to create a plan. What is your timeline? What do you need to do in order to make this happen? Do you need to update your resume? Go back to school? Take an online class or begin to network? You need to start with the goal and then make a plan to break down the steps. Like the age-old question of how do you eat an elephant? One bite at a time. Create the vision of what you want and then begin to map it out in tiny steps to move forward. Each goal needs its own plan. Learning how to take a big impossible idea and break it into tiny manageable baby steps is how we move ourselves and our world forward. This is how every single nonprofit founder created change for themselves and for all of us. It all started with a goal. It is never too late to have one, there is no expiration date on dreams and goals.

Communication

Once we have a plan for our lives, what do we do with it? Do we sit on it and do nothing? Hopefully not. Usually, once we get excited about something, we share our ideas with our friends and family. We begin to communicate the plan. It can be as simple as walking with a friend and telling them that you are thinking about getting a new job. It can be a written communication on social media communicating about your expertise in a field that you hope to work in. You need to be an effective communicator to get any of your ideas across.

Public speaking seems to universally terrify most people. It is listed as a top ten all-time fear. When we need to get the word out about our plan or goal, we often find ourselves in a position, whether we like it or not, to have to speak in front of an audience. That fear can drive so many people from moving forward with their dreams. Like all fears, they only go away once confronted again and again until the fear eventually subsides. I have interviewed so many amazing people who started incredible organizations and had no choice but to overcome their fear of public speaking.

Being an effective communicator is not only about speaking, but it is actually more about listening. Listening to your peers, your team and everyone around you and taking in the input to move yourself and the community forward. I interviewed an amazing woman named Rachel Doyle, who founded a nonprofit called GlamourGals. Rachel was in high school when she lost her grandmother and realized that fifty percent of seniors were living in isolation. To honor her grandmother, she decided to change that. Her idea was to empower beautiful connections between generations. GlamourGals does this by organizing teen volunteer chapters in high schools and colleges to visit local senior homes to provide companionship, conversation and our signature complementary beauty makeovers. The real vision is to end elder loneliness. Rachel has now been doing this work for over twenty years and we recently talked about her work and leadership evolution.

Rachel's Story: Effective Communication

I created GlamourGals when I was a teenager. It was an idea to honor my grandmother who had passed away. Being a teenager, I wanted to do something I enjoy. I think where the success comes in, is this idea of tapping into what's relevant to your audience. I loved fashion, beauty and makeup, so I thought why not? Take the things that I love, my friends love and use it as a tool to make someone smile.

I remember it was August of 1999 that I was thinking of the idea. In January of 2000, I held my very first GlamourGals makeover, and I begged two friends from my homeroom basically saying, "You need this for college, don't you?" I dragged them into the senior home that day. I remember being unprepared for the next question, after the experience they turned to me and said, "Hey, when are you coming back?"

So, the GlamourGals makeover experience is just a vehicle for conversation that's familiar. When you can tap into things that are relevant and provide opportunities for teens to do something and put their own spin on it. I think that's what I'm most proud of is, how we built the organization through this chapter system. Yes, it starts with the manicures and makeovers of the GlamourGals signature programming, but then we give the team leadership of the chapters flexibility through our chapter creativity fund. There they have an idea, and we encourage them to pitch us their idea. Then, we'll give you the materials to go and do that. As a result, they can own a little bit of their local ideas.

In our leadership model for our teens, we give them the opportunity to reflectively journal. The idea is that they go out and do this incredible intergenerational experience and they come back and get training and mentorship from us. Then we give them the chance to write about it and reflect on it. We prompt them to do that all the time, and we've collected over 10,000 reflective journals.

We share them, as an office, on social media to inspire others. Receiving those is really what drives me. On the days where I'm like, "Am I doing something that still makes an impact?" I see what that girl in Ohio or that guy in Texas writes about how much GlamourGals has transformed their life, personally and academically. It is all these stories that we amassed. It's not my journey anymore. It's thousands of other people's journeys. That is just so cool and just so inspiring to me.

Rachel has used her communication skills to build GlamourGirls, but more than that, she has taught these girls to listen to themselves through journaling. GlamourGals has been about creating human connection for 20 years. She said, "During *the pandemic, we had an AI group, run all these fancy technology tests on the Reflective Journals and look for keywords and we found the most popular word in the selected journals was hope. To us, this signaled something really incredible, that during the largest mental health crisis for teenagers, they were coming onto our site and talking about hope. And I think there is something really transforming there. Going back to the core of our program is human relationships, creating for teens transformations that inspire their personal, academic and future professional success.*

The last couple of months, we have started 20 new chapters. We're in a growth period right now with 89 chapters across the country. When everything shut down, one of the programs we launched was called My Dear Friend. It was a card writing program that allowed us to write cards to the seniors in the senior homes and for them to receive something tangible, slipped underneath the door, because there was 100% isolation. Since the launch of that program, we have distributed 100,000 cards around the country and even in foreign cities around the world."

Leading an organization from a teenager to adulthood, for two decades, there was bound to be an evolution in leadership. Rachel reflected upon her own journey when she told me, *"I think I had to recognize that it's okay for my role to change. I've done this for over 20 years. I started off as a volunteer doing the direct service as a team, going into multiple senior homes and going to different classrooms to convince other students to do the same thing. Later on, in college, there were other chapters of young people replicating the service in different communities.*

I remember sitting in a professor's office and she said, "This is a moment where your role has changed, and you have to accept it. You have to move forward in it. Just reflect on this for a moment, you are allowing maybe a thousand other people to do the service by your actions. You may no longer be doing the one action of going into the senior homes, but you're putting the time towards inspiring and organizing a thousand others. You have to see the value in that."

So it was then that the next evolution of leadership came along, and it wasn't just me alone. I had to welcome other people in and be okay with sharing that delegation of power and responsibility. Again, it was allowing and embracing those changes in my leadership role and understanding how I fit into the organization each step of the way."

Rachel understood each of her roles and her evolution as a leader. I think she summed it up best when she said, *"The most important lesson is to be a good listener. As a founder I've been at plenty of meals with people who just talk about themselves. Who wants to be around somebody who just talks about themselves? I think I learned alongside my volunteers to remember to sit down and listen to someone else. Whether it's a senior citizen, a volunteer, a peer colleague or a friend, you just sit, listen, and get to know what they need. When you can understand the needs around you, you can better serve those needs."*

Mentorship- Bre's Story

It is often said that real leaders create other leaders. How do we do that? We teach and mentor one another. In our organization, our college students teach and mentor our high school students. Our high school students teach and mentor our middle school students. We all need mentors and people in our lives who help show us the way or teach us something new. More than having mentors, we need to be mentors. We need to take someone under our wings and help them out, show them the way and who they can become.

A few years ago, I interviewed an amazing young woman named Bre Russell, who started a nonprofit called Girls Leading Girls. The organization trains girls and women in leadership advocacy and life skills through soccer. Bre told me, *"I always knew I wanted to be an entrepreneur. That was always something that appealed to me. I worked at a young age because we were just trying to survive as a family. We didn't grow up with a lot of money, and I relied on a lot of people to help. My coaches making soccer even possible for me was huge. As a result, I wanted to pay it forward and help others."*

Bre realized that there were not enough women coaches or mentors for these young girls and set out to solve the problem by creating an organization to do just that. She said, *"There's definitely a lack of representation of women in sports at all levels. Eight years later, we're starting to see that change. When will we have women as not just referees and athletes, but owners of these higher-level clubs and teams? The challenge is there are not enough women coaches.*

We are recruiting, training and mentoring women to become coaches, even though most never thought they could. There are psychological barriers going up against the male-run old, traditional model of coaching. We are trying to create something different because the old traditional model really was a disservice to girls. Girls drop out of sports at young ages; the statistics are there. Did you know that girls drop out of sports by age 12? That is over 50% more than boys do."

When you realize the power of having a mentor, you want to pay it forward and be a mentor. Bre's words and work amplify that message. She said, *"To see them start with me and then develop from a young age into confident, strong, young women on and off the field is just amazing. I mean, this is the beauty of kids that grow so fast. You can see that growth right before your eyes.*

For example, there's one girl, who was not having great experiences at other organizations that were soccer-focused. She's a very talented athlete, and she took a year off from playing because she was not thriving on these other teams. Her friend, who was playing with us, encouraged her to join our organization, which she did. I felt an instant connection with her because we had similar backgrounds. Her family was just trying to survive, she often had to take care of her younger siblings at a young age. She didn't have a lot of resources or support.

I would pick her up and take her to practice. For the last two years, she improved so much in her soccer skills, and in her leadership, that she was awarded goalie of the year. Today, she's now a paid coach for us and she's playing soccer at SF City College. I just made it my job to support her and see her through this and be her mentor. Obviously, I can't do that for all 700 Girls we serve, but I can model it and be an example, so other coaches will want to do it, too."

This is exactly the power of mentorship. I've had incredible mentors in my life, but in the past twelve years, it is in fellow nonprofit founders that I have found incredible guidance and wisdom. These remarkable humans remind me each week in our podcast conversations of the power of having a mentor at any age. So many of my mentors have become friends, and their sage guidance and wisdom have enriched my life in invaluable ways. It also reminds me that I must pay it forward and mentor others.

Servant Leadership- Ian's Story

At the true core of every leader is someone who serves. You can not lead unless you serve. We so often think of leaders as those people at the top of a triangle yelling down orders to everyone below them. When in reality, true leaders lead from behind bringing their team with them in service. I see these young servant leaders at TACSC, giving their time and their summer to volunteer as counselors to serve other students. The cycle of goodness repeats itself.

TACSC isn't the only organization teaching these invaluable life skills. Last year, I interviewed a really inspirational leader named Ian Sandler. Ian and his wife tragically and unexpectedly lost their nine-year-old daughter, Riley, and knew they wanted to honor her legacy of kindness by creating a world full of kind leaders. They named the organization Riley's Way, and it is a national nonprofit that invests in supporting the next generation of confident leaders. They provide young people with leadership training, coaching, funding and the community that they need to thrive, develop into kind leaders and make a difference in the world. Riley's Way works with emerging leaders, ages 13 to 22, who've started Social Impact organizations in areas like food insecurity, homelessness, equity, and education and environmental justice, all through the lens of kindness, empathy, and human connection. The organization has supported more than 3,000 young people across the country with over $2 million in grants and programs.

Ian and I discussed our mutual goals of teaching students to give back and make a difference in the world. Ian said, *"Our overarching goal is taking the world out 30 or 40 years, and just instilling kind leaders everywhere. It's fuel from all this time with these incredible change makers and seeing the way they're going to go out into the world and look at everything in a different way than they perhaps otherwise would. It just instills this theory of change, which is Riley's vision of having kind friends everywhere. So that's what we're shooting for. And we're gonna keep going. We already think we've got it right with this next generation of kind leaders. We think we have the next Fortune 500 CEOs, the next senators, the next teachers, the next doctors, we need these folks everywhere. You need this approach to kind leadership so that you can really counterbalance this incredibly divisive landscape. We need to get back to this notion of community where we look out for one another, we look out for our planet, and we really have to think about this in a much different way."*

When we teach students to think about others, there is a shift in them. The same thing happens to adults because we find purpose in serving something bigger than ourselves. This service brings purpose, and the purpose brings meaning to our lives. At the end of the day is what we are all actually searching for, the reason we are here and our life's purpose.

I asked Ian what he had learned in doing this work with Riley's Way and his answer was, *"I feel like I'm able to just recognize what really does matter. Being surrounded by people you love and making an impact in people's lives. What I'm able to realize nine years into this is just what matters in life. All these things that I used to think were worries, they were not. Don't overthink it, because life's gonna throw so much stuff at you. And by the way, that really starts with yourself. You can't be good to your family, to your friends, to your colleagues, if you're not in a good place. You have to figure out what that recipe is so that you can then go out and shine for others. I definitely try to do one thing every day that is just purely joyful for me. And I kind of just float through life as a result of all this. So much of it is just the love and the joy we get from this work and community and knowing that you're working for a purpose... I really do feel like I've found my life's purpose."*

There are so many valuable life lessons from Ian, Bre and Rachel. Each of them is a leader and lives a life full of purpose. All three of these nonprofit founders have evolved in their own leadership roles and like all real leaders do, they have grown more leaders. Bre taught us about the importance of mentorship and how we not only strengthen our own skills but bring others up with us. Rachel reminded us of the value of communication and, most importantly, listening to those you serve. Ian is not only developing other young kind leaders and supporting them, but in the process, he is giving the seed money to hundreds of new social impact organizations and nonprofits. These three leaders are perfect examples of how real leaders develop other leaders and the importance of each of us working to improve our own leadership skills.

When we use our gifts for the greatest good and share them with others, that is our purpose. It is that simple. Finding our gifts and giving them away. In the past decade, working with tens of thousands of student leaders, I have seen firsthand the evolution of leadership. Generation after generation, leader after leader, these students learn to make a plan and follow their dreams. They break down the steps to achieving those dreams. These young leaders communicate their plans. Then, they mentor others in the process. Most importantly, each volunteer gives of themselves to change the life of another. They serve. You can feel the love, the kindness, the joy, the gratitude between our campers and our volunteer staff. Regardless of what is happening in the world, I know that our amazing college and high school volunteers are transforming hundreds of children's lives for the better. Each of our volunteers renews my faith in humanity. Every leader I meet, whether they are in 6th grade or they are established nonprofit founders, inspires me to strive to serve more, do more and be more.

Reflection

1. Do you consider yourself a leader? Why or why not?
2. What are some places in your life when you have been a leader? (Your home, school, sports teams, office)
3. What leadership skills did you use in those roles from above?
4. Have you ever had a dream, a goal or a vision that you have not pursued? If so, why not? What small step could you take to move that dream forward?

CHAPTER ELEVEN

Living a Life of Purpose and Action

"I believe purpose is something for which one is responsible; it's not just divinely assigned."
—Michael J. Fox

We are all here for a reason. Each of us has a purpose to be on this planet, and for many of us, we have no idea what that is. We go through each day as zombies, repeating the same actions that we did the day before and the day before that. There is no passion or excitement about the privilege it is to be alive. The reason is we are lacking purpose. As Mark Twain famously said, *"The two most important days in life are the day you are born and the day you find out why."* He was right, it is that purpose that brings meaning, joy and gratitude into our often mundane lives.

When you think about what you are excited about, that is your passion. That passion is the road you need to walk down to find your purpose. It isn't a straight route there. Finding your purpose can be a windy and long path, with many twists and turns along the way. My path has most definitely not been a direct one. Many of my friends believe that their purpose was to be a parent. I adore my sons but never believed that to be my purpose. I believe that I have been the privileged custodian of three amazing young men, but they are not my purpose, and each of them has their own purpose as well.

The Journey Begins with Loss

My path to purpose began with loss and the kind of grief that consumes you to your core, where you come through the experience of loss gutted, fragile and ready to begin again. The process is long and slow and requires faith—blind faith that you are going to survive. Faith is believing in something bigger than you that is going to see you through the journey until you arrive at your destination and your purpose. Faith is that lifeline in rough seas that gets you through the darkest of days and tells you that you will survive even when you aren't sure you will.

Loss and grief have a profound way of reshaping our perspectives, often bringing into sharp focus what truly matters in life. When we lose someone dear to us, it feels as if the world has paused, allowing us to reflect on our priorities. The daily worries and minor irritations that once consumed us seem insignificant compared to the deep connection and love we had for the person we lost. This period of grief is painful, but it also strips away the superficial, leaving us to cherish and value the moments and relationships that make life meaningful.

In the midst of grieving, we often find ourselves reevaluating our lives and the way we spend our time. The hustle and bustle of everyday life, filled with its myriad of distractions, suddenly feels less important. Instead, we become more present, seeking comfort in the simple joys and the people around us. This reset can lead to a more intentional way of living, where we prioritize our loved ones, nurture our relationships, and appreciate the beauty in the ordinary. Grief teaches us that life is fragile and fleeting, urging us to focus on what truly brings us happiness and fulfillment.

Ultimately, the experience of loss can guide us towards a deeper understanding of ourselves and our purpose. It can inspire us to live more authentically, to express our love and gratitude more freely, and to pursue what genuinely matters to us. While the pain of losing someone never fully disappears, it can transform us, making us more compassionate and attuned to the preciousness of life. In the face of grief, we learn to hold tighter to what is essential, finding strength and solace in the connections that endure.

Listening for the Way

During the time of wandering down this path blindly, you have to rely on your other senses, and that means sharpening your listening skills. You must listen, really listen, to the voice of your soul telling you which way to go. That inner voice will always tell you the way if you are quiet and still enough to hear. That voice is your inner compass, and it knows the way. It is your GPS, but the volume is turned down so low that you have to be quiet to hear the directions.

My favorite book is Paul Coelho's *The Alchemist* and it has a quote that discusses the importance of listening to your heart. He says, "*Why do we have to listen to our hearts? Because, wherever your heart is, that is where you will find your treasure.*" Listening to your own voice and to yourself is crucial for finding your path and treasure. When we listen to ourselves, we maintain a healthy and balanced life. Often, we get caught up in the noise of external opinions and expectations, which can drown out our inner voice. By taking the time to tune into our own thoughts and feelings, we can better understand what truly matters to us and make decisions that align with our authentic selves. This self-awareness helps us navigate life with more clarity and confidence.

Furthermore, listening to yourself fosters self-compassion and self-care. It allows you to recognize your own needs, emotions, and limits, which is essential for maintaining mental and emotional well-being. When you honor your own voice, you give yourself permission to rest when you're tired, to speak up when something bothers you, and to pursue activities that bring you joy. This practice of self-listening cultivates a kinder relationship with yourself, which can significantly enhance your overall quality of life.

Embracing your own voice empowers you to live a more fulfilled and purposeful life. When you listen to yourself, you are more likely to follow your passions and dreams rather than conform to societal pressures or expectations. This authenticity not only leads to greater personal satisfaction but also inspires those around you to do the same. By being true to yourself, you contribute to a world where individuality is celebrated, and people are encouraged to pursue their unique paths. This is change for good.

The Obstacle as a Gift

When you cannot see or hear yourself clearly, there will be plenty of obstacles that you will stumble upon on this journey towards purpose. They will feel enormous and insurmountable. These boulders will block your path, try and break you and get you to give up your quest. The obstacle is the way and those roadblocks are actually road signs to head in another direction. When we look back at our lives, we can see clearly where something that we were devastated by ended up being a gift. As Tony Robbins said, *"The problems will come, there's no doubt about that. But the way that I choose to meet them, that is my superpower."*

When you encounter a huge obstacle, and you will, you are well on your way towards purpose and finding your reason for being here, your holy grail. It is a quest, a mission, a journey and the destination will forever change your life. Finding out why you are here and what gifts you have to give and share is what the human experience is all about. It is a path that each of us must walk. We all have different lessons to learn from these paths and each challenge and obstacle is a gift that leaves us wiser.

Have you ever had a huge challenge you didn't think you could overcome? Then, when you did it, you looked back and you were so grateful that you pushed through, so proud of yourself for having gone through the experience? That gratitude is exactly what happens after we overcome something. It could be a physical challenge, a death, a move, a new job, a divorce, whatever the obstacle, we can choose to come through feeling grateful for having survived it.

Finding the Gratitude

The reality is that there is beauty, even in loss and adversity, if we choose to look for it. That beauty is called gratitude. Looking in my own rearview mirror in the twenty-plus years since my parents' car accident, I can now find the beauty in the loss. Would I do anything to see my mom again? Of course, I would. Now, with the clarity of hindsight, I can see that the Spiritual Care Guild would have never happened without that loss. Hundreds of thousands of patients, families and staff wouldn't have had someone at the hospital for them when they needed someone if there hadn't been loss. There was beauty and purpose that came from the loss. While it isn't always clear in the beginning, it is there if we look.

This observation is not just mine, but hundreds of other nonprofit founders who have experienced loss and used their pain as fuel for good. Almost a decade ago, I interviewed an amazing woman named Jo Ann Thrailkill. She had been a successful record producer when her very young son Pablo was diagnosed with pediatric cancer. The loss of a child is the greatest pain and loss for anyone. Jo Ann's friends had started a fund while Pablo was sick, and she and her husband knew they needed to do something positive with this fund after Pablo lost his battle with the disease. JoAnn told me, *"I went to see Pablo's doctor to get direction, and he asked me, "What would you have wanted that you didn't have when Pablo was sick?" And my answer was a cure. So, I knew we were going to need to invest in research since pediatric cancer research is so underfunded: Only 4% of cancer research funding goes towards childhood cancer.*

He then asked me what Pablo would have wanted, and I knew it was something in the arts. I knew that Pablo just wanted to feel like a kid when he was sick and that his photography had been a form of self-expression. So that is how we began the Shutterbugs program which teaches children and teens with cancer the art of photography. Today, The Pablove Foundation has funded more than $3.8 million dollars in pediatric cancer research.

"This entire experience has been completely life-altering for me. I think one of the major things I took away from my own family's cancer experience was that just when you think the world is filled with darkness and hate, you discover that it is actually filled with love. Things don't always end up how you hope or plan that they will, but when we were in the trenches of treatment with Pablo, we discovered the most amazing support from our community and everyone around us. This gave us not only the financial support but also the emotional strength that we needed to start the Pablove Foundation. The experience of starting Pablove has allowed me to always see the light. I am now reminded daily of the love that surrounded me during one of the most difficult times in my life."

The Community

Our journeys can feel overwhelming, lonely and isolating. It is in bringing everyone together in a community that we create our power and healing knowing that we are not alone and that other people care. Bringing people to walk the journey with us is part of the process. That human connection that we crave radiates healing when we walk in the community. When we came together to help Father John, we created a community that didn't exist, but that was united in purpose to help the families and patients at CHLA to have faith in a time of need. We built a community around a common goal. Like bees in a hive, we all hummed together to achieve the task at hand.

Our country was founded on taking care of your neighbor. Being an active member of our towns, schools, churches and being there for our neighbors. Our communities once were our foundations. At the core of nonprofits is community. Healthy nonprofits create thriving hives of activity where all the members work very hard to support the members of their group. Healthy communities do the same. Lately, it seems that our communities seem to be suffering. As a result, our world is too. We need to not lose sight of our local needs and care for those in front of us first.

What would our world look like right now if each one of us took care of our own local tribe? If we were actively involved with helping those in our own communities with jobs, food, education and support? If everyone supported each other at a local level, the need for global support wouldn't exist. This may seem like an oversimplification and perhaps it is. When you think about it, it makes sense.

Community makes us feel connected. It makes us feel safe. Our mental health is stronger because we have that feeling of belonging to a group. Community gives us that safety net that tells us someone is looking out for us. However, today people look to the government for that feeling rather than looking next door. We live in neighborhoods where we don't know our neighbors. Do we know the names of the people who work at our local market? These tiny threads of kindness are what strengthen the fabric that keeps us together.

When these threads are cut our connections erode, then isolation sets in, which is usually followed by fear. Sadly, the result of fear brings the innate need to self-protect rather than the need to reach out to others. We become overwhelmed and shut down. That fear can erode so much goodness. We lose faith in one another, and distrust becomes a cancer that destroys our connections.

As humans, we are meant to be connected, to support one another like bees in a hive. We all have a job and a role to make our communities stronger by working together. Fear robs us all of the honey and the sweetness of feeling connected. When we all take baby steps towards knowing our neighbors, teachers, grocers and the people in our communities, we become stronger. We need to strengthen our neighborhoods by getting together. Support our schools and places of worship. Get involved! If each of us takes these tiny steps to make our own communities stronger, as a result, we become more unified. Ultimately, we make our world a better place, one community at a time. It all starts with us.

Leadership

Once we are in our communities, we begin to see places where our gifts can help others. When we identify those gifts and put them to use, that is when we naturally begin the process of leadership. You don't start your journey trying to lead, you simply just want to find out who you are and why you are here. In the process of learning the answers to those questions, that is when you discover your leadership.

For the past twelve years, I have been privileged to serve over 25,000 students in their leadership formation. In 2013, the students that we taught were in middle school, and today are in their twenties. To witness these young leaders' development has been one of the greatest privileges of my life. It is this same transformation that I see year after year, generation after generation, leader after leader, of young students changing the world that has kept me doing this important work. It gives me hope to see our students learn about goal setting, communication (the old-fashioned in-person kind with real handshakes), becoming mentors and serving others. It all sounds so simple and basic, but it is so much more.

I know if these young students can make this evolution, you can too. Each student starts with a goal and a dream of what they want. They then learn how to communicate that dream, and in the process, they create a community of people around them who support them in achieving their goals. These students mentor other students and inspire the next generation of leaders. Most importantly, these young leaders learn that you can not lead unless you serve. Becoming a servant leader and using your gifts to help others is what makes us leaders.

I am grateful for the gift of this work, which does so much good for our world. It has been a gift to witness kindness, empathy, faith, compassion, and leadership. We have never needed kind, good moral leaders more than now. I continue to be grateful for the tens of thousands of <u>TACSC</u> leaders making a difference in our world each day. These young leaders affirm my belief in the importance of each of us learning to lead and serve.

Purpose

Now that we are back to purpose, our journey has come full circle. Once we walk the path to purpose, we know each of these stepping stones along the way we must touch upon to get there. Shortcuts are not an option, and the path is long. Like a recipe, there are no shortcuts: all the ingredients must be in the formula to make it work. You forget one, and you will not achieve the desired outcome.

We are all given such a tiny amount of time on this planet. Don't we want to know everyday that we used every precious moment to achieve something? That our lives mattered? That we were here, and the world is somehow a tiny bit better because we existed? Isn't that the reason why we are here? We are all here to learn from our journey the lessons along the way. That journey is our path towards purpose. Our purpose is to serve one another. We need to find our gifts and bring them to the hive in service. That is nirvana, the holy grail, the entire point of our lives.

As Winston Churchill once said, *"It's not enough to have lived. We should be determined to live for something."* That something is our purpose to use our time here on earth to leave it a little better than we found it. Whether it was our impact on our family and children, our careers, the kindness we gave to others, our generosity or how we served. That is the change we must go through to create change for good.

Spreading the Light

You would think that now you have gone through this wild journey towards your purpose that your work would be done. However, you have a new role once you have completed the path and that is to enlighten others to help them to understand the journey and to use your gifts to help as many people as you can. I know there are days when we are empty and feel that we do not have enough to give, and that is ok. We can not give all the time. When we keep our cup full from the lessons above, that is when we have enough to give to others. That is when we know we have created change for good, not only within ourselves but within our families, our communities and our world.

The crazy thing about service is that the more you give, the more you receive. It sounds impossible, but that is exactly how it works. The most fascinating thing is that when we set out to serve, we are not looking to receive but rather to give. To help a cause, be a part of something bigger, volunteer in our children's classrooms, and the list goes on as to why we serve. We do these actions for a variety of motives but thinking about what we get from giving is never one of them.

What is so fascinating is that as the years roll by and the service continues, grows and expands, so does what comes back. I have served in so many capacities in my five decades and all with different motivations. Serving is an evolution and a process, just like the journey we described above. As a young girl, I served because I was told to. As a teen, I served because that's what my friends were doing. In college, I served because it was a great way to meet people and do something nice for someone. As a young mother, I served to make new mom friends and to begin to teach my children about giving.

It was only later, when I was overwhelmed with grief, lost and bereft, that service healed and saved me. Like a lifeline to a drowning victim, service was there to rescue me as I was going under from grief. Service pulled me from my despair and showed me so many others whose lives were in need. Being able to help families at Children's Hospital Los Angeles not only healed my grief but it gave me a new purpose.

Now decades later, it sounds so cliché to say you get what you give, but honestly, you get so so much more. My life is beyond abundant; I could have never dreamed of this journey. I ask God each day to use me towards my greatest purpose as I continue to strive to serve. It is a privilege to know that you have used your life to make others better. Truly, the greatest gift of all.

Reflection

1. In reflecting on your own life journey, where on the path do you see yourself?
2. Do you think you walked on each stone of the path? Loss, listening, obstacles, gratitude, community, leadership and purpose?
3. Is there one missing? If so, which one and why?
4. Do you think you have found your purpose yet?
5. If so, what is it?
6. If not, what steps do you need to take to get there?

CHAPTER TWELVE

Are You Ready?

"Use your life to serve the world, and you will find that it also serves you." —Oprah

Life teaches us many lessons, and we are all here to learn. Oftentimes, the harder the lesson, the more pain we have had working through it. When we look back at our lives and see those challenging and painful moments, those are the periods of huge growth. The phone call that changed my life, a car accident, a death, and nothing was simply ever the same after that call. That loss became my superpower.

I think many of us feel that growth comes in tiny layers added up over time and that each day's journey gets us a little closer to inner-growth. I have a different theory. I believe life is like an earthquake where huge jolts cause cataclysmic shifts like tectonic plates to our souls. In nature, these shifts result in mountains. Inside each of us is a similar experience. When the rocking stops, we somehow come out shifted. Our vision becomes clearer, we see what is important for the first time, we learn gratitude in everything, and the growth is as monumental as a mountain. It is the growth of our soul.

Each setback is a gift and a lesson. Do we all look at these horrible losses as gifts? Probably not. We react as if they happened to us and not for us. These obstacles are our lessons, and each lesson is a gift of growth. When we lose someone we love through death, divorce or moving away, we do not immediately think of this sadness and pain as a gift. It hurts, and all we can process is the emotion of sadness, and that's ok. Once we begin to work through the emotion and we sit and listen to ourselves, that is when we begin to hear the lesson from this loss.

In the past twelve years, I have been privileged to have had many teachers on this subject. Unlikely teachers at that, nonprofit founders, entrepreneurs and modern-day heroes who have walked a similar path to mine with their pain and have turned it into purpose. These wise men and women have inspired me with each interview and life lesson. It is my hope that by introducing you to a few of them in this book, you have gained some of their insight and wisdom as well.

We are all handed pain in this lifetime. It is our shared human experience and the school of life we all attend. We are here to learn from this pain and then take that wisdom to change for good. First, the change must be within, and ultimately, when our cups are full, our change can become in service of others. I have a sign above my desk that reads, *"What good shall I do today?"* It is my daily reminder that I am not here to serve myself but to use my life to serve others to the best of my abilities.

What's in Your Toolbox?

Trust me, as I said in the beginning of this book, there is no halo here, and while I hope to make it on the A train to heaven, I am no saint. My sailor's mouth alone is going to get me stopped at the pearly gates for sure! I am not advocating saintly behavior, although one could try. What I am asking is for you to look at your gifts and ask yourself how to best use them to help others. After years of work, I have realized that my gifts as a communicator are what tools I was given to work with. I use those tools to be a messenger of service through the Charity Matters blog, podcast, social media, public speaking, my work at TACSC and now with this book.

What I am asking you is, what is in your toolbox? What gifts have you uncovered through journaling and reading this book? Hopefully, you have allowed yourself quiet time to listen to yourself, to reflect, to hear your inner voice speak to you. Maybe through reflection, you have discovered that you have a passion for gardening, and maybe you could work with schools to develop their gardens or work on an inner city garden? Maybe you are gifted with music and could sing or play an instrument at a home for the elderly? The options for your gifts and matching the needs of others are endless.

The challenge is that we do not think about our gifts as things to give away. It doesn't just have to be the money that we give. The greatest gift we have is our time and our talent, so why don't we start with giving those first? Think about your gifts. You are an accountant, an attorney, an artist, a baker, a marketer, an organizer, whatever it is you do for a living, there is a gift in that skill. It is a gift that someone can use. When we think about volunteering, so many things come to mind. Working at a soup kitchen, stuffing envelopes or doing something menial, but that is not the case. There is a match for a nonprofit that needs just the gift you have. Giving doesn't need to be menial, it needs to be joyful.

Where Do I Start?

Where and how do I start? Once you have figured out what you are good at and you know your gifts, now the fun part is to begin to think about where to give them away. You don't want to give your gifts to just anyone; hopefully, there is a cause you care about. What is your magis? Magis is the Latin word for more. What makes a fire burn in your belly? Let's start with that. What do you care so deeply about that you need to do more? Was it that family member that you lost to breast cancer or driving by a homeless encampment or your high school or college? Maybe you have a specific cause you care about, but it's a big topic, like the environment or education. The next step is to narrow your focus and begin to think about what piece of those topics specifically is exciting to you. Maybe it's time to do a little research on the topic and the organizations that support them.

Then, it's time to ask yourself a few questions. What change do you want to see? Do you care about the rainforest, or are you worried about the literacy rate in America or your city? Starting to understand the problem that you want to address and learning about it will let you know if this is still exciting to you and something you want to know more about and get more involved with. We need to understand the problems before we can begin to identify solutions and how we can be a part of them.

As you continue your research into nonprofits that support your cause, begin to look at the programs that they offer. Ask yourself how those programs solve the problem and bring change. When we are taking on some of the world's biggest problems, like homelessness, for example, there are many different ways that organizations offer solutions. Some organizations might provide job training, while others, like the nonprofit Miracle Messages, attack the problem by creating human connections through their phone buddy program. So think about which programs speak to you.

The bigger the problem, the slower the change and the longer it can take to see an impact. Jenny and Josie Hull's hospital room makeovers offer instant gratification for the teen volunteers seeing their work appreciated by young patients. Solving a problem like breast cancer research can be slow. Ask yourself where you will see change and who will benefit from this change. Will your work help raise awareness? Then ask yourself what the timeline is that you are looking for. Maybe you need something more immediate than a long-term project. There are no wrong answers, but asking yourself these questions will help set you up for success with whichever path you pursue.

Think of these 1.6 million nonprofits with open jobs and imagine that you are looking for a job. These, of course, are not paying jobs, but they are jobs or projects. You would go to either an employment center, online to a job board and try to find a paid job that matches your skills. The same thing exists in the nonprofit space for volunteers, and it's called catchafire.org. Think of it as LinkedIn for nonprofits. You can go onto their site and list your skills as an attorney, graphic artist, accountant, marketing or whatever you may be and then list what causes excite you. For example, say that you love animals and are a graphic designer. You can list your skills and the causes you are interested in, and they will match you with a project from a nonprofit creating graphics for a new fundraising campaign. These projects can be a few weeks or longer, and most are remote and some in person. It is an incredible way to try on a cause, meet new people and build your resume while making a difference.

I have recommended this platform for years, and they do a really great job of matching people to causes. There is zero downside, and this is definitely where you should start if you don't already have a cause you care deeply about. There are other sites that have more traditional volunteer work, like VolunteerMatch.com, where you can put in your zip code and be given a wide range of opportunities in your area, which is a terrific way to meet people in your community and make a difference. This is another great place to begin to dip your toes into the giving-back pool of joy.

These opportunities exist at every age. It's never too early to start. There are sites for children like kidsthatdogood.com to find ways that they can give back. The earlier our children start, the greater the reward. When our boys were younger, each Thanksgiving, we would have them propose something they were interested in—animals, the military, learning to read—then we would vote on a cause to sponsor that year, or at minimum, that holiday. We adopted families, soldiers for a year (my boys loved sending letters and care packages) and, over the years, had a variety of different experiences. All enriched their lives, opened their eyes and hearts and made them into the empathetic men they are today.

Jenny and Josie's Story:

My youngest son was good friends with two darling girls who started a nonprofit while they were in high school. The girls were on a mission to do extreme hospital room makeovers for children who had serious health challenges, and they recruited my son, along with hundreds of other teenagers, to join their mission with their nonprofit Once Upon a Room. Jenny and Josie are a perfect example of a family using their gifts to serve others. Jenny told me, "*I worked with an amazing family in Malibu, and they were very involved in an organization called Healing the Children. Subsequently, I became involved with them too. What we did there was bring kids here to the United States for surgeries, and then we'd send them back home after they were healed.*

We got this request for these two adorable high-conjoined twin little girls. It was kind of our mission to bring these babies, Josie and Teresa, here to America, and they were conjoined at the head. They were separated at UCLA Medical Center and had a 23-hour surgery. Our girls were the first successful girls to be separated successfully. Long story short, I am now the very, very proud adoptive mother of Josie, one of the twins. Josie's other twin is with another amazing family in Valencia, and we're really close. The birth parents are really the heroes in the story, selflessly allowing their children to be in America because that's the only way they would have survived. They really are the unsung heroes in this, we are so grateful to them.

I can't even count the number of days and surgeries, there have been too many! Every time Josie had surgery, we personalized her room to make her feel special and comfortable. Everybody would walk in, look at it, and say,

"Oh my gosh, Josie, you love pink!" Then, they would recognize her as a person instead of what she was there for, and it really touched our hearts.

We realized it was especially important in a teaching hospital when you have so many new residents, for them to recognize the patient as a person. So at 11 years old, we were laying in bed one night, and I vividly remember Josie leaned over and said, "Mom, I really really need to be doing something for someone else. I want to help other kids in the hospital." I said, "That's a great idea!" We called Sienna, Josie's best friend, who was the same age and told her the idea. Sienna said, "Let's go in and decorate these hospital rooms." Then, Sienna came up with the name, Once Upon a Room.

In all honesty, we thought when we started we'd do 50 rooms a year at CHLA. Period. We thought this is great, and it's something that will inspire the girls, and they can inspire other people. We didn't think much of it, and we ended up doing 105 rooms our first year. Our town is so supportive. They really rallied behind what we were doing and really supported the effort and we were so grateful for that.

Then, we started expanding, and all of a sudden, it was like the universe opened. Because the girls took this on, people saw the greatness and what it did for the hospital's families and especially patients.

We started in one hospital at CHLA in Southern California. We are now in 19 hospitals across the country. It continues to grow; we've done over 4000 rooms.

Primarily the impact we have on the kids and their families with their hospital days and medical journeys, but more than that, we have such an impact on the volunteers, the hospital staff, and our donors. I have had friends who have come to the hospital to volunteer, in high school and college, not knowing what they want to do when they grow up and leave saying, "Oh, I know, I want to be a nurse, or I want to be a child life specialist." One volunteer is now working in the foster care system because she met people through her work with us at the hospital. So, I think it's everybody around that really is affected by it, not just the patient or family. It's everybody involved.

Sienna (who was in college when we spoke) told me, *"Walking into kids' rooms every day who were super sick or at the end of life made me realize how lucky I am just to be healthy. I think it's something that we all take for granted. So that's something that I quickly learned, talking to these kids, watching them fight for their lives, watching them lose their battles to cancer; it was really hard to watch. But it made me so grateful for everything that I have.*

It also taught me, from a young age, how important it is to give back and to help other people. I feel like it's a really great gift that I got from Jenny and Josie that I learned that this was something that made me feel so good and made me feel like I was doing something to help other people. And it's something that I continue to do. I know, I'll take it with me wherever I go. Prioritizing, helping other people, giving back, brightening someone's day, even if it's something small. You never know what kind of difference that you can make."

Jenny, Josie and Sienna are perfect examples of why it doesn't matter what age you are when you start as long as you start. Josie had been a patient so many times and knew what cheered her up, having a hospital room that looked like her bedroom at home. She wanted to give back to children who didn't have that. They each knew what gifts were in their toolboxes and wanted to use them for others. Jenny not only knew how to create impactful relationships with people at the hospital and was extremely crafty, she knew how to decorate and make everything look beautiful. Sienna is an organizational powerhouse, and together, they all used their unique gifts and talents to serve others. The girls were barely teenagers when they started their nonprofit with Jenny's amazing oversight and vision. Their story is a reminder that it is never too late or too early to start giving back.

Change for Good

Change for Good is about the journey that each of us must walk in our own unique way. It is our life's mission to find out why we are here. What do we care about, and how do we want to make our world better? It is living a legacy life and not a resume one. Do you want to be remembered for your career or how you made others feel? What values do you have that you want to live out? We have so many opportunities to make a difference with our time and our lives.

The first decision is to make the choice, and if you are reading this book, my guess is that you already have. Choosing to serve and help others is no different than choosing to go on a diet. You must research that meal plan and what food choices you are going to make to enact your new lifestyle. Choosing to serve is a similar path. Once you make the choice and do the research about where and how, you are off to the races. The choice is more than deciding to serve and who to help. The change for good is making choices on what matters and having your time and attention follow what is important to you.

It is time to focus on people who change the world by following these inspirational humans on social media rather than the latest reality star. Time to make choices about what media and news we consume. Choosing to follow things that inspire us and lift us up. Reading and spending time on topics that mean something to you rather than just flipping on the TV to the news or whatever is on. These are choices that keep our cups full. It is choosing to be with people who lift you rather than put you down. These choices create change for good. It is when we make these choices that we are able to finally use our gifts to make another's life better. That is how we all change for good. It is the change within us that matters the most. Then, it is taking that change to our communities and igniting it in others.

The reality is that our lives, our families, our communities and our world are NOT someone else's problem. It is ours. We can not be passive bystanders in our lives and in our communities. If we want things better then we need to take action, even if in the smallest step. We must act. The Catholic school I attended from kindergarten through high school's motto was Actions Not Words. That motto has served me well, regardless of how much I like to talk. We can not sit on the sidelines of life and be armchair quarterbacks, we must jump in and play the game. We must act!

Serving others allows you to leave a lasting legacy that extends far beyond your own lifetime. The impact of your acts of kindness can ripple through generations, inspiring others to follow in your footsteps and continue the cycle of giving for years to come. The benefits of serving others are multifaceted; physical, mental, social, career and having a greater purpose. By embracing a lifestyle of kindness and generosity, you not only enrich the lives of those around you but also experience a profound transformation within yourself.

Your acts of kindness can open a new world of fulfillment rooted in your desire to connect with a greater purpose. Every time you help someone or volunteer, you move closer to realizing the significant impact you can have on others' lives. These actions will make you feel genuinely useful and grateful to those who inspired your philanthropic spirit.

When we set aside our desire for recognition and embrace selflessness, we embody the purpose we chose before birth. Doing what we love for others, rather than for personal gain, maximizes the talents the universe has given us. Giving makes us feel most useful and shows we can positively change lives. There's no need to doubt our skills when we see their impact. Your kindness will help you fulfill your inner needs by allowing you to live your destiny.

By giving in to our compassionate impulses, we contribute to a larger movement to improve the world. From small acts of charity to large missions of kindness, our efforts counteract the suffering around us. Brightening the lives of those we serve creates a ripple effect of contentment. Those we help are likely to help others, spreading compassion further. As you act charitably, you become part of the positive change you wish to see.

We are all here to serve one another and on a mission to discover what gifts we have to do that. Our lives are serendipitous journeys that teach us lessons along the way. Mine took me from caring to loss, a rebirth, being healed through service, meeting modern-day heroes, and through it all, learning to lead and now teaching young leaders. That journey brought me here to you at this moment. How wonderful the journey is when we open our hearts to serve.

Life has a funny way of coming full circle to teach you lessons and to connect all the dots...like a final exam to make sure you were paying attention to the lessons along the way. They say everything you need to know you learned in kindergarten. I know I did. As Mrs. Thompson said, "When you give and expect nothing, that is when you receive the most."

So, now what? Now, it's time to go out and use those tools and gifts you were given for good. You are a person with vision, communication, mentorship and service. Most importantly, you care and that is your invitation to change the world for good.

Fun facts on people changing the world for good

- There are a staggering 1.5 million nonprofit organizations in the United States alone
- The first nonprofit organization began in the United States in 1657. The Scots' Charitable Society as the oldest charitable organization in America. It was founded to aid Scots who were captured by English forces and sold as indentured servants. They are still helping their fellow Scots today.
- Nonprofit organizations employ 7.4% of the worldwide workforce.
- 70% of these workers are paid and 29% are volunteers.
- 5.7% of the United States GDP comes from nonprofits
- The United States annual revenue for nonprofits is a staggering $2.63 trillion dollars
- 56% of Americans donated to charity in 2021
- One in four Americans volunteer.
- That equals 4.1 billion hours or $122.9 billion dollars.
- Women volunteered more than men by a few percentage points.
- Baby Boomers gave the most time, then Generation X followed by sixteen and seventeen Gen Z at 28%

Benefits of Giving

- Report by Angela Thoreson on the Mayo Clinic website said that, "Volunteering improves the physical and mental health of adults over 60 and lowers the rates of depression and anxiety for those over 65."
- 2020 in the Journal of Happiness Studies, researchers examined data from nearly 70,000 research participants in the United Kingdom. These participants received surveys about their volunteering habits and mental health from 1996 to 2014.

Those who volunteered at least once a month reported better mental health than participants who volunteered infrequently or not at all.

- A 2012 study by the University of Michigan determined that older people who volunteer with regularity tend to live longer than those who don't, but only if your intentions are altruistic

Footnotes/Sources

Sources:

Candid Learning. How many nonprofit organizations are there in the US? | Knowledge base | Candid Learning. Accessed on March 14, 2022.

- Independent Sector, The Charitable Sector. Accessed on March 14, 2022.
- The Nonprofit Times. 7.4% Of World Workforce In Nonprofits. Accessed on March 14, 2022.
- National Center for Charitable Statistics. The Nonprofit Sector in Brief 2019 | National Center for Charitable Statistics. Accessed on March 14, 2022.
- Statistica. • US nonprofit organizations: revenues 2016 | Statista. Accessed on March 14, 2022.
- Blackbaud Institute. Online Giving Trends – Blackbaud Institute. Accessed on March 14, 2022.
- Philanthropy News Digest. Nonprofits Are America's Third Largest Employer, Study Finds | Philanthropy news | PND. Accessed on March 14, 2022.
- Foundation Group. 50 Nonprofit Facts and Statistics. Accessed on March 14, 2022.
- LendingTree. 56% of Americans Donated to Charity in 2021, at an Average of $574. Accessed on March 14, 2022.
- Double the Donation. Nonprofit Fundraising Statistics [Updated for 2022]. Accessed on March 14, 2022.
- The Nonprofit Times. 80% Of Nonprofits' Revenue Is From Government, Fee For Service. Accessed on March 14, 2022.
- National Philanthropic Trust. Charitable Giving Statistics – NPTrust. Accessed on March 14, 2022.

- Philanthropy News Digest. Online giving up more than 20 percent in 2020, report finds. Accessed on March 14, 2022.
- Statistica. • US nonprofit organizations: number 2016 | Statista. Accessed on March 14, 2022.
- BLS. Nonprofits account for 12.3 million jobs, 10.2 percent of private sector employment, in 2016: The Economics Daily: US Bureau of Labor Statistics. Accessed on March 14, 2022.
- Nanoe. Nonprofits Fail – Here's Seven Reasons Why. Accessed on March 14, 2022.
- Forbes. America's Top 100 Charities. Accessed on March 13, 2023.
- Independent Sector. Health of the U.S. Nonprofit Sector Quarterly Review. Accessed on March 13, 2023.
- https://teamstage.io/volunteering-statistics/
- *(source: Volunteering and Civic Life in America research.)*

Change for Good:
The Transformative Power of Giving

We hope *Change for Good* has inspired you to go out and make a real difference! Our mission is to create a movement of people who are ready to help others in meaningful ways, both big and small.

We'd love for you to be part of it. Our mission is to create a movement of doers who lean in to help one another in ways big and small. You can start by signing up for our weekly newsletter at www.Charity-Matters.com. Each week, we'll introduce you to inspiring everyday heroes who show how living with purpose can bring so much joy. Plus, you'll get access to our **Charity Matters** podcast, along with practical tips and ideas to help you build a sense of community and make lasting change.

Thank you for believing in what we're doing. Together, we can make the world a better place, one small act of kindness at a time.

Meet the Author
Who Turned Pain into Purpose

Heidi Johnson is a nonprofit founder, storyteller, and believer in good. She uses the power of connection to bring people together through her work in the nonprofit sector.

For the past decade, Heidi has communicated powerful stories to inspire service through her blog and podcast, Charity Matters while serving as the Executive Director of a Youth Leadership Organization.

Heidi is one of the founders of the non-profit, Spiritual Care Guild at Children's Hospital Los Angeles, where she is a past Trustee on the hospital's board and the Spiritual Care Advisory board. She has been recognized for multiple service awards including the Cardinal's Award, the highest recognition of service in the Archdiocese of Los Angeles.

Heidi's work has been published by Thrive Global, Medium, and Conscious Magazine and she has a monthly column about making a difference in FORCE Magazine. She is a first-time author with her new book, *Change for Good*. Heidi and her husband are the very proud parents of three incredible sons.

When tragedy struck Heidi Johnson's life, she was unsure how to survive the overwhelming grief. But through her journey of healing and service, she encountered stories of ordinary people facing extraordinary challenges, who nonetheless found ways to make meaningful contributions to society. In "Change for Good," Heidi shares these inspiring stories and shows us that the capacity to serve others lies within each of us, waiting to be tapped into for the greater good. With heartfelt guidance and practical wisdom, Heidi offers a roadmap for transforming pain into purpose and finding joy in giving back.

Heidi's Mission statement

"I believe in the power of connection to bring people together for a purpose greater than themselves. I believe in communicating powerful stories to inspire others to serve and give. I believe in planting the seeds of compassion in our youth, most specifically to serve. I believe you cannot lead unless you serve. My mission is to inspire others to serve. We all have the power to change our world when we simply help one another."

Social media links

Website: https://charity-matters.com
Instagram: @CharityMatters and @HeidiJohnsonOffical
Facebook: https://www.facebook.com/CharityMattersLA
Linkedin: https://www.linkedin.com/in/heidi-mcniff-johnson-7758b225/
Twitter: @Charity_Matters
Youtube: https://www.youtube.com/@CharityMatters/featured
Spotify for Podcast-
https://podcasters.spotify.com/pod/show/charity-matters

www.ingramcontent.com/pod-product-compliance
Lightning Source LLC
Chambersburg PA
CBHW071359120626

46546CB00002B/753